Good Housekeeping DESSERTS from A to Z

All pictures by James Viles except the following, courtesy of The National Magazine Company, Ltd.: Orange Souffle, Chocolate Eclairs, Peach Snow Mold, Grape Delight, Classic Puff Pastry, Queen of Puddings, For Chocolate Lovers, Petits Fours. Recipe on page 158 from *Charleston Receipts*, courtesy of the Junior League of Charleston

Good Housekeeping
DESSERTS
from
A to Z

Good Housekeeping Books
New York

Good
Housekeeping
DESSERTS
from
A to Z

ANGEL-FOOD CAKE

1 cup plus 2 tablespoons cake flour,
sifted before measuring
1½ cups sifted granulated sugar
1¼ cups egg whites,
at room temperature (10
to 12 eggs)
¼ teaspoon salt
1¼ teaspoons cream of tartar
1 teaspoon vanilla extract
¼ teaspoon almond extract

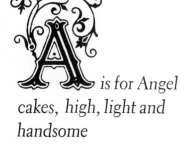

is for Angel cakes, high, light and handsome

Several hours before serving: Preheat oven to 375° F. Sift flour with ½ cup of the sugar 4 times. In large bowl, combine egg whites, salt, cream of tartar, extracts. With electric mixer at high speed, beat egg whites until stiff enough to hold soft, moist peaks. Beat in remaining 1 cup sugar, ¼ cup at a time; beat just until sugar is blended. Stop mixer. Sift in flour mixture by fourths, folding in each addition with 15 complete fold-over strokes of spoon, rubber spatula, or wire whisk, turning bowl often. After all flour has been folded in, give batter 10 to 20 extra strokes.

Gently push batter into ungreased 10-inch tube pan. With spatula, cut through batter once.

Bake ½ hour or until cake tester inserted in center comes out clean. Remove from oven; turn pan upside down. Do not remove cake until cool.

ORANGE: After sifting flour with sugar, add 3 *tablespoons grated orange peel*; toss with fork. Substitute *1 teaspoon orange extract* for vanilla and almond extract.

GALA RAINBOW DESSERT

1 15- or 16-ounce package
angel-food cake mix
2 cups heavy or whipping cream
¼ cup sifted confectioners' sugar
1 16-ounce can apricot halves,
drained and mashed
1 16-ounce can crushed pineapple,
well drained
green food color
¼ cup thick raspberry jam

Early in day: Prepare cake mix as label directs for 10-inch tube pan.

Whip cream until stiff; stir in sugar. Fold ½ cup of the whipped cream into mashed apricots, ½ cup whipped cream into pineapple (tint delicate green), and ½ cup whipped cream into jam. Cut cooled cake into 4 even layers. On bottom layer, spread apricot filling. Place second layer on top; spread with pineapple filling. Top with third layer; spread with raspberry filling. Top all with fourth layer; spread top and sides of cake with rest of cream; sprinkle outer top edge with slivered, toasted almonds if desired. Refrigerate. Makes 12 servings.

MOCHA ANGEL SPECIAL

1 15- or 16-ounce package
angel-food cake mix
1 cup butter or margarine
1⅔ cups sifted confectioners' sugar
dash salt
1 teaspoon vanilla extract
2 egg yolks
2 1-ounce squares unsweetened chocolate,
melted
instant coffee
2 egg whites, stiffly beaten
2 cups heavy or
whipping cream

Day before: Preheat oven to 375° F. Prepare cake mix as label directs. Pour into two 9″ by 5″ loaf pans; bake 35 to 40 minutes; cool. Freeze one cake.

Meanwhile, make filling by creaming together butter and confectioners' sugar. Add salt, vanilla and egg yolks; beat thoroughly. Add chocolate, ⅓ cup water, 2 teaspoons instant coffee; beat well; fold in egg whites. Cut cake into 4 even layers. On serving plate, assemble layers with filling between; refrigerate.

Several hours before serving: Add 1 tablespoon instant coffee to cream; whip until stiff; spread over top and sides of cake. Refrigerate at least 3 hours, then cut into slices. Makes 8 to 10 servings.

CHOCOLATE-SWIRL ANGEL-FOOD CAKE

Several hours before serving: Prepare *one 15- or 16-ounce package angel-food cake mix* as label directs. Pour one fourth of cake batter into ungreased 10-inch tube pan. Grate *two 1-ounce squares unsweetened chocolate;* sprinkle one third over batter. Repeat, alternating batter and chocolate and ending with batter. Bake as label directs.

LAYERED ANGEL-FOOD CAKE
pictured between pages 16-17

1 16-ounce package lemon-custard
angel-food cake mix
1 3¾-ounce package
chocolate pudding-and-pie filling
1 1-ounce square unsweetened chocolate
¼ cup rum
1½ cups heavy or whipping cream
yellow food color

Day before serving: Prepare cake mix as label directs. Pour into 10-inch tube pan.

Meanwhile, using ½ cup less milk than called for, make up chocolate pudding as label directs. Place piece of waxed paper directly on top of pudding; refrigerate. Using vegetable peeler, make curls from chocolate.

Remove cooled cake from pan; cut into 3 even layers. Around top outside edge of cake plate, lay four 2-inch waxed-paper strips in a square. Place bottom layer, cut side up, on plate. Sprinkle cut surface with 2 tablespoons of the rum; spread with half of chocolate pudding. Now top this layer with second layer; sprinkle with remaining rum, then spread with remaining pudding. Top with third layer, crust side up.

In large bowl, whip cream until stiff; fold in a few drops of yellow food color. Spread on top and sides of cake; sprinkle chocolate curls around sides of cake. Remove waxed paper strips; refrigerate.

At serving time: Cut cake into 16 wedges; serve each on dessert plate. Makes 16 servings.

P.S. If you prefer, you may bake the cake and make the chocolate filling the day before. Then fill, frost and decorate cake a few hours before serving, refrigerating it until needed.

CHERRY ANGEL JUBILEE

Early in day: Make *two 10-inch angel-food cakes*. Cool. Cut each cake into 12 wedges. On large round tray, arrange wedges in large circle, alternating 2 wedges pointing in with 1 wedge pointing out. Frost with *1 quart heavy or whipping cream*, whipped. Refrigerate.

Just before serving: In skillet, melt *1½ cups currant jelly*; add *4 drained 17-ounce cans pitted Bing cherries*; heat to simmering. Pour into bowl placed in center of cake. Dip *6 sugar cubes* into *lemon extract*; set upright on cherries; light cubes, then whisk flaming cake to the table. Makes 24 servings. For 12, make half the recipe.

LEMON ANGEL CAKE

1 15- or 16-ounce package
angel-food cake mix
grated peel of 2 lemons
6 tablespoons granulated sugar
1½ tablespoons cornstarch
½ teaspoon vanilla extract
1 tablespoon lemon juice
⅛ teaspoon red food color
6 canned cling-peach slices
3 large strawberries, halved

Early in day: Prepare cake mix as label directs, folding in grated lemon peel. Bake in 10-inch tube pan; cool as label directs. When cool, remove cake from tube pan, then invert on cake plate; cover with piece of waxed paper.

About 2 hours before serving: Make glaze: In small saucepan, mix sugar and cornstarch; add 1 cup water. Cook, stirring, over medium heat, until clear and thickened. Remove from heat; add vanilla, juice and food color.

Arrange peach slices and strawberries on top of cake. With pastry brush, glaze fruit as well as entire top of cake, letting some of glaze drizzle down sides of cake.

Refrigerate, uncovered, until serving time. Makes 12 to 14 servings.

TWIN ANGEL CAKES

1 10-inch angel-food cake
1 envelope unflavored gelatin
2 10-ounce packages
frozen strawberries or raspberries, thawed
4 teaspoons lemon juice
2 egg whites
⅛ teaspoon salt
1 cup heavy or whipping cream
2 cups flaked coconut for garnish

Early in day: Cut angel-food cake crosswise into 2 even layers. Hollow out cut side of both layers, leaving shells not quite 1 inch thick. Place each shell on serving plate. Fill in tube hole in each with bits of cake.

Sprinkle gelatin over ½ cup cold water to soften; stir over hot water until dissolved; stir into berries with lemon juice; refrigerate until partially thickened. Then beat egg whites with salt until stiff. Whip cream; fold into fruit mixture with beaten whites. Refrigerate a few minutes; heap in cake shells. Refrigerate several hours.

To serve: Decorate tops of cakes with coconut. Makes 16 to 18 servings.

PINEAPPLE-PARFAIT CAKE

1 15- or 16-ounce package
angel-food cake mix
2 teaspoons unflavored gelatin
1 20-ounce can crushed pineapple,
drained
2 cups heavy or whipping cream
yellow food color

Day before or early in day: Prepare cake mix as label directs. Pour into 10-inch tube pan.

While cake is cooling, make filling as follows: Over 2 tablespoons water in glass measuring cup, sprinkle gelatin to soften; stir over hot water until dissolved, then stir into pineapple. Refrigerate until almost set. Whip cream; fold 1 cup of it into pineapple mixture. Invert cooled cake; cut into 3 even layers, then fill with pineapple cream.

With food color, tint remaining whipped cream a delicate yellow; use to cover top and sides of cake. Refrigerate at least 3 hours or until serving time. Makes 16 servings.

CHOCOLATE ANGEL DESSERT

1 15-ounce or 16-ounce package
angel-food cake mix
$\frac{1}{8}$ teaspoon nutmeg
2 cups heavy or whipping cream
$\frac{2}{3}$ cup fudge sauce
$\frac{1}{2}$ pound crushed English toffee

Day before: Prepare cake mix as label directs, adding nutmeg to batter; pour into 10-inch tube pan. Bake; cool completely; remove from pan. Cut cake crosswise into 2 even layers. Whip cream until almost stiff; fold in fudge sauce. Frost lower layer of cake with some of cream mixture; sprinkle with some of toffee. Set top layer in place. Frost top and sides with cream mixture; sprinkle with remaining toffee. Refrigerate at least 8 hours. Makes 16 servings.

BERRY BASKET CAKE

1 15- or 16-ounce package
angel-food cake mix
¼ teaspoon grated lemon peel
1 quart fresh strawberries or raspberries
¼ teaspoon lemon extract
½ cup sifted confectioners' sugar
2 cups heavy or whipping cream

Early in day or day before: Prepare cake mix as label directs, folding in lemon peel. Bake in 10-inch tube pan, then cool completely as label directs.

About 1 or 2 hours before serving: Hollow out cake, leaving shell about ¾ inch thick. Place on large serving plate. Fill bottom of center tube hole with piece of cut cake. Tear or break rest of cut cake into bite-size pieces. Wash and hull berries; save about 2 cups of the prettiest ones for garnish; slice rest. Add extract and sugar to cream; whip until stiff. Fold in cut-up berries and broken pieces of cake. Heap high in cake shell (fill center hole too). Scatter whole berries over and around cake. Makes 12 servings.

Freezer Note: Cut leftover cake into serving-size pieces. Freezer-wrap each piece; freeze quickly. To serve, let thaw in refrigerator just until soft.

CHRISTMAS ANGEL FOOD

1 15- or 16-ounce package
angel-food cake mix
¼ teaspoon almond extract
⅓ cup finely chopped toasted almonds
⅓ cup chopped candied pineapple,
drained
2 cups heavy or whipping cream
¼ teaspoon pistachio
extract
green food color

Day before or early in day: Prepare cake mix as label directs, then fold in almond extract, almonds and pineapple. Bake in 10-inch tube pan as directed; cool. Remove cake from pan; cut into 3 even layers.

Whip cream; fold in pistachio extract. With food color, tint cream a delicate green; fill and frost layers. Chill. Makes 12 servings.

is for Bavarian creams and their cousins, soufflés

BAVARIAN CREAM

1 envelope unflavored gelatin
dash salt
granulated sugar
2 eggs, separated
1¼ cups milk
1 cup heavy or whipping cream
1 teaspoon vanilla extract

Day before: In double-boiler top, combine gelatin, salt, 2 tablespoons sugar. Slowly stir in egg yolks and milk. Cook over boiling water, stirring, until mixture coats spoon. Refrigerate until slightly thickened.

In small bowl, with electric mixer at high speed, beat egg whites until they form moist peaks when beater is raised; gradually add ¼ cup sugar, beating until stiff. Fold into yolk mixture. Whip cream, fold with vanilla into yolk mixture. Leave in bowl; or turn into 1½-quart mold. Chill.

To serve: Unmold or spoon into sherbet glasses. Nice as is, or topped with flaked coconut and green crème de menthe. Makes 6 to 8 servings.

MOLDED CHEESE BAVARIAN

2 envelopes unflavored gelatin
1 cup granulated sugar
¾ teaspoon salt
2 eggs, separated
1 cup milk
2 teaspoons grated lemon peel
3 tablespoons lemon juice
3 cups cottage cheese
1 cup heavy or whipping cream
halved, peeled orange slices
and small bunches of grapes

Day before: In double-boiler top, mix gelatin, sugar, salt. Beat egg yolks with milk; stir into gelatin. Cook over boiling water, stirring constantly, until mixture thickens and coats spoon.

Cool mixture. Add peel, juice and cheese; with rotary beater, beat until well blended. Refrigerate until mixture mounds slightly when dropped from spoon.

In small bowl, with electric mixer at high speed, beat egg whites until stiff. Whip cream. Fold gelatin mixture into egg whites; fold in cream. Turn into 2-quart mold or 8 sherbet glasses. Refrigerate.

To serve: Unmold onto large dessert plate. Garnish mold or sherbet glasses with orange slices and grapes. Makes 8 to 10 servings.

CRANBERRY BAVARIAN

1 pound cranberries
2 cups granulated sugar
3 tablespoons grated orange peel
2 envelopes unflavored gelatin
½ cup orange juice
4 egg yolks, beaten
1 cup milk
1½ teaspoons vanilla extract
1 5-ounce package shortbread cookies,
crumbled (about 1½ cups)
1 cup finely chopped walnuts
¼ cup butter or margarine, softened
2 cups heavy or whipping cream

Early in day: In large saucepan, combine cranberries, 1½ cups of the sugar, orange peel and 1 cup water; boil until skins of berries pop, about 5 minutes. Force mixture through food mill; set aside.

In cup, soften gelatin in juice. In double-boiler top, stir yolks with remaining ½ cup sugar and milk. Cook over simmering water, stirring, until mixture thickens, about 15 minutes. Remove from heat. Stir in vanilla and gelatin, stirring until dissolved. Cool 5 minutes. Gradually stir into cranberry puree. Chill, stirring occasionally, until mixture mounds when dropped from a spoon.

Combine crumbs, walnuts and butter. Grease bottom and sides of an 8-inch springform pan and spread ⅓ crumb mixture in bottom of pan.

In large bowl, with electric mixer at high speed, whip cream until stiff peaks form; carefully fold in cranberry mixture. Carefully pour half of mixture into pan, making a smooth layer. Sprinkle with half of remaining crumbs; repeat layers. Refrigerate.

To serve: Remove outer rim of springform pan; cut in wedges. Makes 10 servings.

ALMOND SOUFFLÉ

3 3½-ounce packages vanilla-flavor
whipped-dessert mix
1 cup heavy or whipping cream
5 teaspoons almond extract
canned diced toasted almonds

Day before or early in day: Prepare 4-cup-capacity china soufflé dish with foil collar as in step 2 of Baked Orange Soufflé (page 20).

In large bowl, with electric mixer at high speed, prepare whipped-dessert mix as label directs. Refrigerate. Whip cream, then fold cream and almond extract into whipped-dessert mix. Pour into soufflé dish; refrigerate at least 4 hours or until firm.

To serve: Remove foil collar from soufflé; pat diced almonds into sides of soufflé that stand above rim of dish. Makes 12 to 15 servings.

COLD COFFEE SOUFFLÉ
pictured between pages 16-17

3 cups coffee
1 cup milk
3 envelopes unflavored gelatin
6 eggs, separated
granulated sugar
½ teaspoon salt
1 teaspoon vanilla extract
1¼ cups heavy or whipping cream
1½ teaspoons confectioners' sugar
grated peel of 2 oranges

Day before or early in day: In double-boiler top, combine coffee, milk, gelatin; scald, while stirring occasionally, to dissolve gelatin.

In small bowl, with electric mixer at medium speed, beat egg yolks with 2 tablespoons sugar and salt until thick and lemon-colored.

To egg yolks, with mixer at low speed, gradually add some of hot coffee mixture, blending well. While stirring, pour this egg-yolk mixture back into rest of hot-coffee mixture in double boiler.

Cook over very hot, *not boiling*, water, stirring constantly, until mixture thickens slightly and coats spoon. Pour into large bowl; refrigerate, stirring occasionally, until small amount mounds when dropped from spoon, about 1½ to 2 hours.

Meanwhile, prepare 6-cup-capacity china soufflé dish with foil collar as in step 2 of Baked Orange Soufflé (page 20).

In large bowl, with electric mixer at high speed, beat egg whites until frothy; gradually add 1 cup sugar and vanilla, beating until stiff. Fold into gelatin mixture and beat smooth.

Whip 1 cup of the heavy cream; fold into gelatin-egg-white mixture. Pour into prepared soufflé dish; refrigerate.

At serving time: Carefully remove foil collar from around soufflé. Whip remaining ¼ cup heavy cream with confectioners' sugar until stiff; use in decorating bag, with large tube number 2, to garnish soufflé. Pat grated peel around sides of soufflé; sprinkle some on top. Makes 12 servings.

COLD SOUFFLÉ GRAND MARNIER
pictured between pages 16-17

granulated sugar
Grand Marnier
2 tablespoons lemon juice
1 envelope plus 2 teaspoons
unflavored gelatin
7 eggs, separated
½ cup candied mixed fruits, drained
¾ cup canned diced, roasted almonds
2½ cups heavy or whipping cream
¼ teaspoon salt
2 preserved kumquats, cut in 4 wedges

Day before serving: In medium saucepan, combine ½ cup sugar, 1 cup water, ½ cup Grand Marnier, lemon juice, gelatin, egg yolks. Cook over low heat, stirring, until mixture coats spoon and gelatin is dissolved. Transfer to large bowl. Refrigerate until like unbeaten egg white.

Meanwhile, soak finely cut-up candied fruits in 2 tablespoons Grand Marnier. Prepare 7½-cup-capacity china soufflé dish with foil collar as in step 2 of Baked Orange Soufflé (page 20).

Into cooled gelatin mixture, fold ½ cup of the almonds and fruits.

Whip 2 cups of the cream. In large bowl, with electric mixer at high speed, beat egg whites with salt until they form soft peaks; gradually add ¼ cup sugar, beating until stiff. Fold both into gelatin mixture, then turn into soufflé dish. Refrigerate.

About 20 minutes before serving: Sprinkle remaining almonds around top of soufflé. Carefully remove foil.

Whip remaining ½ cup cream until stiff; use in decorating bag with large pastry tube number 6 to garnish as pictured. Dot kumquats over whipped cream. Makes 10 servings.

RASPBERRY CREAM SOUFFLÉ
pictured between pages 16-17

4 10-ounce packages frozen raspberries,
slightly thawed
granulated sugar
3 envelopes plus 2 teaspoons
unflavored gelatin
2 tablespoons lemon juice
7 egg whites
¼ teaspoon salt
4 cups heavy or whipping cream

Day before: Prepare 7½-cup capacity china soufflé dish with foil collar as in step 2 of Baked Orange Soufflé (page 20).

Reserve 10 raspberries for garnish (wrap in foil; refreeze). In medium saucepan, with fork, crush remaining berries; add ¼ cup sugar, 3 envelopes of the gelatin and lemon juice. Stir over medium heat until gelatin dissolves. Chill over ice cubes, stirring constantly, until mixture just mounds when dropped from spoon; pour at once into 3-quart mixing bowl.

In large bowl, beat egg whites with salt until they form soft peaks; gradually add ¼ cup sugar, beating until stiff.

Sprinkle remaining gelatin onto ¼ cup water; dissolve over hot water. In large bowl, combine cream, 2 tablespoons sugar and dissolved gelatin; beat until stiff. Fold half of whipped cream and egg whites into cooled raspberry mixture. Refrigerate 1 cup of remaining whipped cream. Spoon raspberry mixture into soufflé dish, to rim. Make two layers each of remaining whipped cream and raspberry mixture. Chill 1 hour.

Carefully remove foil collar. Put reserved whipped cream in decorating bag with large pastry tube number 6. Press cream on top of soufflé as pictured. Refrigerate.

Just before serving: Garnish with reserved berries. Makes 16 servings.

PINEAPPLE-AVOCADO SOUFFLÉ

2 envelopes unflavored gelatin
6 eggs, separated
1 cup granulated sugar
1 teaspoon salt
1 tablespoon grated lime peel
½ cup lime juice
1 8¾-ounce can crushed pineapple, undrained
3 avocados, peeled and mashed
1 cup heavy or whipping cream, whipped

About 5 hours before serving: Prepare 1½-quart soufflé dish with foil collar as in step 2 of Baked Orange Soufflé (page 20). Sprinkle gelatin over ½ cup cold water to soften.

In double-boiler top, combine egg yolks, ½ cup of the sugar, salt, lime peel and juice. Cook over boiling water, stirring constantly, until thickened. Stir in gelatin until dissolved. Remove from heat; stir in pineapple and avocado; refrigerate until slightly thickened.

In large bowl, beat egg whites until soft peaks form. Gradually beat in remaining sugar until stiff peaks form. Gently fold in whipped-cream-and-avocado mixture. Pour into soufflé dish. Refrigerate at least 3 hours or until firm.

Just before serving: Remove foil collar. Makes about 10 servings.

Layered Angel-Food Cake, page 8 —fluffy lemon layers put together with creamy chocolate filling

Five Cool Masterpieces: Clockwise, Cold Soufflé Grand Marnier, page 15; Marble Bavarian

This light and lovely Orange Soufflé, **page 20**, waits for no man; serve it as soon as it's baked

ORANGE SOUFFLÉ BRÛLÉE
pictured between pages 16-17

1 cup orange juice
sherry
granulated sugar
3 teaspoons grated lemon peel
3 tablespoons lemon juice
1 envelope plus 2 teaspoons
unflavored gelatin
7 eggs, separated
1 3-ounce package ladyfingers,
cut into large pieces
1 cup cut-up orange sections
2 cups heavy or whipping cream
¼ teaspoon salt
3 tablespoons light brown sugar
15 whole blanched almonds

Day before serving: In medium saucepan, combine orange juice, ½ cup sherry, ½ cup granulated sugar, 1 teaspoon of the grated lemon peel, lemon juice, gelatin and egg yolks; stir smooth. Cook over medium heat, stirring constantly, until mixture coats back of spoon and gelatin is dissolved. Transfer to large bowl. Refrigerate until cool and the consistency of unbeaten egg white.

In small bowl, place cut-up ladyfingers; over them pour ⅓ cup sherry; let soak a few minutes.

Meanwhile, prepare 7-cup-capacity china soufflé dish with foil collar as in step 2 of Baked Orange Soufflé (page 20).

Into cooled orange-sherry mixture, fold sherry-soaked ladyfingers and cut-up orange sections. Whip cream until stiff.

In large bowl, with electric mixer at high speed, beat egg whites with salt until they form soft peaks, then gradually add ¼ cup granulated sugar while beating until stiff peaks form.

Into orange-sherry mixture, carefully fold whipped cream and beaten egg whites; turn into soufflé dish; refrigerate.

Early in day: Preheat broiler 15 minutes (it has to be very hot). Meanwhile, sprinkle brown sugar over top of soufflé and insert almonds here and there. Brown quickly, close to high heat, just one-half minute. Refrigerate until chilled.

Before serving, carefully remove foil. Gently pat remaining 2 teaspoons grated lemon peel around sides. Makes about 10 servings.

For 5 servings: Use only 4 eggs and 2½ teaspoons gelatin with half as much of the other ingredients. Turn mixture into 6-cup-capacity china soufflé dish, omitting foil collar. Chill. Broil with same amount of brown sugar and almonds.

MARBLE BAVARIAN SOUFFLÉ
pictured between pages 16-17

3 envelopes unflavored gelatin
8 eggs, separated
granulated sugar
1 tablespoon vanilla extract
¼ cup all-purpose flour
1 quart milk
4 1-ounce squares semisweet chocolate
4 tablespoons cocoa
about 6 drops yellow food color
2 cups heavy or whipping cream
¼ teaspoon salt

Early in day: Sprinkle gelatin over 1 cup cold water to soften.

In large saucepan, combine egg yolks with ¾ cup sugar and vanilla extract; blend in flour, stirring until smooth; add milk; blend well. Cook over medium heat, stirring constantly, until custard coats back of spoon. Remove from heat. Add gelatin mixture; stir to completely dissolve. Refrigerate, stirring occasionally, until small amount mounds when dropped from spoon.

Meanwhile, prepare 10-cup-capacity china soufflé dish with foil collar as in step 2 of Baked Orange Soufflé (page 20). In small saucepan over hot, *not boiling*, water, melt semisweet chocolate.

Divide cooled custard mixture in half, placing each half in large bowl. Into one half, stir melted semisweet chocolate and cocoa until smooth. Into other half, stir yellow food color.

In a large bowl, with electric mixer at high speed, beat egg whites with salt until they form soft peaks; gradually add ¼ cup sugar, while beating until stiff. Whip cream. Into chocolate mixture, fold half of whipped cream and half of beaten egg whites. Into yellow mixture, fold rest of cream and egg whites.

Into soufflé dish, alternately spoon yellow and chocolate mixtures. Then, with rubber spatula, cut through mixture several times, swirling light and dark batters in marbleized effect. Refrigerate.

Just before serving: Remove foil from soufflé. Makes 16 servings.

OMELETTE SOUFFLÉ

About ½ hour before serving: Preheat oven to 400° F. Generously grease 17½-inch heatproof platter, or 1½-quart oval skillet, or 10″ by 6″ glass baking dish; sprinkle with *1 teaspoon granulated sugar.*

In large bowl, with electric mixer at high speed, beat *5 egg whites* until stiff and shiny, but still moist. Over them, gradually sprinkle *3 tablespoons granulated sugar*, while beating until sugar is dissolved and egg whites form peaks when beaters are raised.

In small bowl, at same speed, beat *4 egg yolks* until thick and lemon colored, while adding *1 or 2 tablespoons granulated sugar*, depending on sweetness desired. Lightly, but completely, fold this mixture into whites. Then spoon this omelette-soufflé mixture onto greased platter, mounding it around sides, with a depression in center.

Bake 18 to 20 minutes or until puffed and well tinged with brown. Remove from oven at once; sprinkle with a bit of *granulated sugar;* spoon *strawberry jam* into center; rush to table. Makes 4 to 6 servings.

HOT CHOCOLATE-VANILLA CLOUD

5 1-ounce squares semisweet chocolate
⅓ cup heavy or whipping cream
4 egg yolks
granulated sugar
2 teaspoons vanilla extract
¼ teaspoon salt
1 cup milk
2 tablespoons cornstarch
5 egg whites at room temperature
soft vanilla ice cream

About 1½ hours before serving: Prepare 6-cup-capacity china soufflé dish with foil collar as in step 2 of Baked Orange Soufflé (page 20).

Into small shallow roasting pan, pour 1 inch of water; set in oven. Preheat oven to 350° F.

In double-boiler top, over hot, *not boiling,* water, melt semisweet chocolate; remove from heat. Stir in cream. Pour into soufflé dish; with rubber spatula, spread some of the chocolate partially up sides of dish in 7 or 8 scallops; keep rest of dish free of chocolate.

In bowl, with electric mixer at high speed, beat egg yolks with ¼ cup sugar, vanilla and salt until light and lemon colored. In saucepan, blend milk into cornstarch. Bring to boiling over high heat, stirring constantly; boil 1 minute. Remove from heat; gradually add to egg yolks, beating constantly. Beat until smooth.

In large bowl, with electric mixer at high speed, beat egg whites until foamy. Gradually add ¼ cup sugar, beating to soft peaks. Fold egg-yolk mixture into whites. Gently pour over chocolate layer.

Set soufflé in pan of water in oven. Bake 1 hour, or until set. Remove from oven; quickly remove collar. Serve at once, spooning to bottom of soufflé for sauce; pass ice cream. Makes 6 servings.

BAKED ORANGE SOUFFLÉ
pictured between pages 16-17

1 or 2 oranges
4 tablespoons Grand Marnier
1¼ cups crumbled ladyfingers (about 8)
1⅓ cups milk
⅓ cup all-purpose flour
2 tablespoons butter or margarine
granulated sugar
4 egg yolks
5 egg whites
confectioners' sugar

1. *About 1½ hours before serving:* With vegetable peeler, remove several thin slivers of peel from one orange; cut enough thin strips to make 1 tablespoon; reserve. Into bowl, peel and cut enough orange sections to make ¾ cup; drain and reserve 2 tablespoons juice. Add orange sections to ladyfingers with 3 tablespoons of the Grand Marnier. Preheat oven to 400° F.
2. Fold 30-inch length of foil, 12 inches wide, in half lengthwise. Wrap around edge of 1½-quart china soufflé dish so a collar, 3 inches high, stands above rim. Fasten with cellophane tape. Generously grease inside of foil collar only.
3. In small mixing bowl, blend 6 tablespoons of the milk with flour. In saucepan, bring rest of milk, butter and ⅓ cup granulated sugar to boiling. With wire whisk, stir flour mixture into milk; beat well. Cook over low heat, stirring constantly, until very thick. Remove from heat and beat in egg yolks, one at a time; add remaining Grand Marnier and reserved orange juice. Return to low heat; cook, stirring constantly, for 2 minutes or until thick. Remove from heat.
4. In large bowl, with electric mixer at high speed, beat egg whites until very stiff; stir ½ cup of the beaten egg whites into egg-yolk mixture, gently fold this mixture back into remaining egg whites; pour half into soufflé dish; cover with ladyfinger crumbs and orange sections; pour on remaining mixture. With back of spoon on top of soufflé, trace a circle 1 inch in from edge of dish. Bake on lower rack of oven for 1 hour without peeking; top will become quite brown, but soufflé needs the full hour of baking.
5. Meanwhile, in small saucepan, simmer orange peel in water to cover about 15 minutes or until tender; drain; add 1 teaspoon granulated sugar to peel.
6. As soon as soufflé comes from oven, remove foil collar; dust with confectioners' sugar; arrange orange peel around edge. Serve immediately. Makes 6 servings.

BUFFET CHEESECAKE

3 10¾-ounce packages
unbaked cheesecake mix
2 tablespoons dark rum
20 canned whole blanched almonds
4 or 5 candied cherries

is for Cheesecake and Chocolate Cake too

Day before serving: In one bowl, make up crumb mixture from 3 cheesecake mixes as label directs. Use this crumb mixture to line bottom and 3 inches up sides of 16″ by 4″ by 4″ loaf angel-cake pan, pressing crumbs firmly and evenly with fingers; freeze.

In large bowl, make up cheesecake filling from the 3 mixes as label directs; add rum; spoon into crumb-lined loaf pan; freeze.

About 20 minutes before serving: Dip loaf pan of cheesecake, almost up to top, in hot water for about 20 seconds. Run metal spatula around sides, all the way to bottom, to loosen. Unmold cheesecake onto serving plate.

Garnish with almonds and cherries . Let stand 15 minutes before cutting. Makes about thirty ½-inch slices.

SUNSHINE CHEESECAKE

1 cup graham-cracker crumbs
⅓ cup packed brown sugar
¼ cup butter or margarine, melted
2 8-ounce packages cream cheese, softened
granulated sugar
¼ cup butter or margarine
¼ cup all-purpose flour
2 eggs
1 cup milk
grated peel of 2 oranges
1½ teaspoons vanilla extract
2 teaspoons cornstarch
½ cup orange juice
3 or 4 oranges, sectioned

Day before or early in day: Preheat oven to 325° F. In small bowl, combine cracker crumbs, brown sugar and melted butter; press into bottom of 9″ by 3″ cheesecake or springform pan; bake 10 minutes.

Meanwhile, in large bowl, with electric mixer at medium speed, mix cream cheese with ¾ cup granulated sugar, butter and flour, mixing until well blended. Add eggs, one at a time, mixing well after each addition. At low speed, mix in milk, orange peel and vanilla. Pour mixture over baked crust. Turn oven up to 350° F., bake 40 minutes or until knife inserted in center comes out almost clean. Remove from oven. Cool completely on rack; remove rim of springform pan.

In small saucepan, combine ¼ cup granulated sugar, cornstarch, orange juice and ¼ cup water. Cook over medium-high heat, stirring constantly until mixture becomes a clear, slightly thickened glaze; cool slightly.

Meanwhile, arrange orange sections on cheesecake in petal design. With pastry brush, brush sides and top of cake with glaze. Refrigerate until firm, at least 4 hours. Makes 10 to 12 servings.

BLUEBERRY CHIFFON CHEESECAKE

1⅓ cups finely crushed vanilla wafers
granulated sugar
2 tablespoons butter or margarine, softened
1 8-ounce container
creamed cottage cheese
1 3-ounce package Neufchâtel cheese
1 envelope unflavored gelatin
1 cup canned pineapple juice
1 teaspoon grated lemon peel
2 tablespoons lemon juice
2 egg whites
¼ teaspoon salt
1 cup canned blueberry-pie filling

Early in day: Preheat oven to 375° F. Mix crushed wafers with 2 tablespoons granulated sugar and butter. With back of spoon, press mixture to bottom and sides of 9-inch pie plate. Bake 7 minutes; cool.

Press cottage cheese and Neufchâtel cheese through a fine sieve, or blend smooth in an electric blender.

In medium saucepan, mix gelatin with ¼ cup granulated sugar, pineapple juice, grated lemon peel and lemon juice. Let stand 5 minutes, then heat until gelatin is dissolved. Add cheese mixture; beat until smooth; refrigerate until slightly thicker than unbeaten egg whites.

Beat egg whites with salt until they form soft peaks, then gradually add ¼ cup granulated sugar, beating until stiff peaks form. Fold gelatin mixture into beaten egg whites; pour into crust; chill.

Just before serving: Spread cheesecake with blueberry filling. Makes 10 servings.

RICH CHOCOLATE-LAYER LOAF

2 16-ounce packages poundcake mix
9 1-ounce squares
unsweetened chocolate, melted
(1 8-ounce package plus 1 square)
4½ cups sifted confectioners' sugar
½ cup hot water
8 egg yolks
¾ cup butter or margarine
about ½ cup canned blanched, sliced almonds

Day before serving: Preheat oven as poundcake-package label directs. Grease 16″ by 4″ by 4″ loaf angel-cake pan.

In one large bowl, prepare the 2 packages of mix together, following label directions. Pour batter into prepared pan. Bake cake 1 hour and 15 minutes or until golden. Cool in pan as label directs; carefully unmold on 2 racks placed end to end; cool completely, right side up, then store.

Early in day: In large bowl, with electric mixer at low speed, combine melted chocolate, confectioners' sugar and hot water; add egg yolks, one at a time, beating at medium speed after each addition. (Refrigerate egg whites for making meringues or other favorites next day.) Now beat in butter, 1 tablespoon at a time; refrigerate frosting until of spreading consistency, about 15 minutes.

Meanwhile, with knife, trim top from poundcake until level; cut loaf into 5 even lengthwise layers. Spread about ½ cup of frosting on each of 4 of the layers; place frosted layers on top of each other, on a serving platter or board of suitable size. Top these layers with the fifth layer, and spread top and sides of loaf with remaining frosting. Arrange almond slices in even rows on top of cake; refrigerate until served. Makes 20 servings.

EASY CHOCOLATE TORTE

2 13½-ounce frozen
chocolate-frosted chocolate cakes
unsweetened cocoa
½ cup heavy or whipping cream
1 1-ounce square unsweetened chocolate

Two hours before serving: Set 1 chocolate-frosted chocolate cake on tray or cake plate. Set second chocolate-frosted cake on top of it, upside down, so two frostings become a filling; press layers together.

Sift cocoa over top of cake until completely covered. Whip cream; place spoonfuls of whipped cream around top edge of cake; grate unsweetened chocolate over the cream. Refrigerate. Makes 12 servings.

SACHER TORTE

5 1-ounce squares semisweet chocolate
½ cup butter or margarine, softened
¾ cup granulated sugar
6 eggs, separated
1 teaspoon vanilla extract
¾ cup cake flour, sifted before measuring
½ cup ground, blanched almonds
¼ teaspoon salt
1 10-ounce jar apricot preserves
Chocolate Glaze (below)
whipped cream

Day before serving: Preheat oven to 350° F. Lightly grease and flour bottom and sides of 9-inch springform pan. In double boiler, over hot, *not boiling*, water, melt chocolate; set aside to cool slightly.

In large bowl, with electric mixer at medium speed, cream butter and ½ cup of the sugar until light and fluffy. Beat in egg yolks, one at a time, keeping mixture fluffy. Gradually beat in melted chocolate and vanilla, then flour, almonds and salt.

In medium bowl, with electric mixer at high speed, beat egg whites and remaining ¼ cup sugar until stiff peaks form; gradually fold beaten whites into chocolate mixture. Pour into pan and bake 50 minutes or until cake tester inserted in center comes out clean. Cool on rack; carefully remove sides of pan. Cover; store.

About 1 hour before serving: Carefully split cake into 2 layers. On cake plate, place bottom layer, cut side up; spread with apricot preserves, then top with second layer, cut side down. Frost cake with Chocolate Glaze; refrigerate. Serve with whipped cream. Makes 12 servings.

CHOCOLATE GLAZE

In double boiler, over hot, *not boiling*, water, melt *1 cup semisweet-chocolate pieces* with *2 tablespoons butter or margarine, 1 tablespoon milk* and *1 tablespoon light corn syrup* until smooth, stirring occasionally. Add a few drops of *vanilla extract.* Use while warm to frost cake.

CAFÉ BRÛLOT

1 orange
whole cloves
1 3-inch cinnamon stick
1 piece lemon peel, 3 inches long
6 lumps sugar
1 cup brandy
¼ cup Cointreau
1 teaspoon vanilla extract
1 quart very hot, strong black coffee

Shortly before serving: From orange, cut a continuous strip of orange peel 1 inch wide; stick it with cloves at 1-inch intervals.

In silver punch bowl or large chafing dish, place orange peel along with cinnamon, lemon peel and sugar.

At serving time: In small saucepan, heat brandy over low heat so that it does not catch fire. Meanwhile, pour Cointreau and vanilla into punch bowl or chafing dish; add very hot coffee. Fill ladle with hot brandy; pour rest into bowl. Light ladle of brandy; slowly pour it, flaming, into bowl. Serve in demitasse, brûlot or diable cups. Makes 8 servings.

is for Drinks that can double as desserts

AFTER-DINNER ICED COFFEE

Several hours ahead: Make 1 quart double-strength regular or instant coffee as below but add ¼ teaspoon anise seed; chill. Make Coffee Ice Cubes, if you like.

Just before serving: Strain coffee into glasses over regular or coffee ice cubes. Spoon a generous serving of *whipped cream* or *frozen whipped topping* on top and garnish with curls of *semisweet chocolate*. Serve as beverage or light summer dessert. Makes four 1-cup servings.

❧ DOUBLE-STRENGTH COFFEE: Brew hot coffee, but use twice the amount of ground coffee as usual. Fill tall glasses with ice cubes and pour in hot coffee. Serve with cream and sugar.

❧ INSTANT COFFEE: In tall glass, dissolve instant coffee with a little warm water. (Use about twice as much instant coffee as you use for a cup.) Fill glass with ice cubes, then cold water; stir. Serve with cream and sugar.

❧ COFFEE WITH COFFEE ICE CUBES: Brew coffee as usual; cool. Pour into ice cube trays; freeze. At serving time, fill glasses with coffee ice cubes. Pour fresh-brewed, regular-strength coffee over cubes. Serve with cream and sugar.

CAPPUCCINO NAPOLI

pictured between pages 112-113

½ cup heavy or whipping cream
½ teaspoon vanilla extract
1 tablespoon granulated sugar
3 to 4 tablespoons instant coffee
2 cups boiling water
ground cinnamon
grated orange peel
sugar cubes (optional)

About 5 minutes before serving: In small bowl, combine cream, vanilla and granulated sugar; whip together until stiff.

Dissolve coffee in boiling water. Divide whipped cream among 5 demitasse cups; lightly sprinkle each with cinnamon and grated orange peel.

Pour hot coffee over cream and serve at once, with sugar cubes, if desired. Makes 5 servings.

QUICK CAPPUCCINO

Just before serving: In medium saucepan, heat *1 cup milk* until hot but not boiling; stir in *3 heaping teaspoons quick chocolate-flavored-milk mix.* Add *3 cups hot double-strength coffee* and *2 teaspoons vanilla extract* or *¼ cup brandy.* Serve immediately. Makes eight ½-cup servings.

QUICKER CAPPUCCINO: Instead of 3 cups double-strength coffee, add *6 heaping teaspoons regular instant coffee* or *4 teaspoons freeze-dried coffee* to 3 cups boiling water.

SPARKLING ICED TEA WITH FRUIT KABOB

Several hours or 15 minutes before serving: In large pan, bring *2 quarts water* to boiling; immediately add *4 level tablespoons loose tea* or *12 tea bags;* let steep 3 minutes.

Stir tea and strain into large pitcher. Cover; let stand until serving time. (Do not refrigerate or tea will become cloudy.)

Just before serving: Pour into ice-filled glasses. Garnish with *Fruit Kabob,* if you like. Makes 2 quarts tea.

FRUIT KABOB GARNISH: On skewers, arrange *one each* of the following: *strawberries, fresh pineapple chunks, orange chunks, quartered limes or lemons.*

EASY-WAY LEMONADE

Early in day: Into large heatproof bowl or pitcher, thinly slice *2 lemons* and add ½ cup *granulated sugar*. Add *2 sprigs fresh mint*, if you like. *Pour in 1 quart boiling water* and stir until sugar is completely dissolved. Chill.

Just before serving: Pour lemonade into 4 tall, chilled glasses and garnish with some of the lemon slices.

SANGRIA

½ cup lemon juice
1½ cups orange juice
½ cup granulated sugar
1 bottle dry red wine (⅘ quart)
1 7-ounce bottle club soda (¾ cup)
½ cup fruit (sliced oranges,
bananas, peaches, lemons, or pineapple)
1 tray ice cubes

Just before serving: Into large pitcher, pour lemon juice, orange juice, sugar; stir to dissolve sugar completely. Add wine and club soda, then mix in fruit. Add ice cubes and serve immediately. Makes eight 6-ounce servings.

ꞔ MOCK SANGRIA: Into large pitcher, pour *4 cups grape juice* and *two 7-ounce bottles club soda*. Add tray of ice cubes; garnish with thin orange, lemon, banana, peach, or pineapple slices. Makes eight 6-ounce servings.

STRAWBERRY SWIRL

3 10-ounce packages
frozen sliced strawberries, thawed
1 quart buttermilk or yogurt

Just before serving: Pour thawed sliced strawberries into 1½-quart pitcher; add buttermilk or yogurt to fill.

At serving time: Stir together, in front of guests, until completely blended; pour into glasses. Guests sip or spoon out the dessert-drink. Makes 8 to 10 servings.

CHOCOLATE-FILLED CREAM PUFFS
pictured between pages 112-113

1 3¾-ounce package
chocolate pudding-and-pie filling
2 teaspoons orange extract
Choux Pastry (opposite)
1 cup heavy or whipping cream
½ cup semisweet-chocolate pieces
¼ cup light corn syrup
¼ cup coarsely chopped
pistachio nuts for garnish

*is for Éclairs
and cream puffs   as well*

Early in day: In saucepan, make up chocolate pudding as label directs, using 1½ cups milk; stir in orange extract. Turn into bowl; place waxed paper directly on surface of pudding; cool. Prepare Choux Pastry as for Cream Puffs (opposite)

Meanwhile, whip cream; gradually fold it into cooled chocolate pudding; chill. In double boiler, over hot, *not boiling*, water, melt chocolate pieces. Stir in corn syrup and 1 tablespoon water. Set aside.

At serving time: With sharp knife, ⅓ of the way down from top, cut off top of each cream puff, crosswise. Hollow out each; spoon in some chocolate filling; replace top. Spoon some of chocolate sauce over each; sprinkle with pistachio nuts. Makes 8 to 10 servings.

CARDINAL PUFFS

½ recipe Choux Pastry (opposite)
2 pints butter-pecan
ice cream
2 10-ounce packages
frozen raspberries, thawed
1 tablespoon cornstarch

Early in day: Preheat oven to 375° F. Prepare Choux Pastry as in steps 1 and 2 of Chocolate Eclairs. Onto greased cookie sheet, drop mixture by heaping tablespoons in 6 mounds, 2 inches apart. Bake until well browned and puffy, about 50 minutes. Remove from oven; at once cut 1 or 2 slits in side of each. Bake 10 minutes longer; cool on rack.

Using number 12 scoop, make 6 ice-cream balls. Place on cookie sheet; freeze. Drain juice from raspberries; place juice in saucepan. Blend cornstarch with 2 tablespoons cold water; stir into juice; cook, stirring, until thickened. Remove from heat; add berries; cover; chill.

About 10 minutes before serving: Slice off top of each puff; fill with ice cream; replace top; top with raspberry sauce. Makes 6 servings.

CHOCOLATE ECLAIRS
pictured between pages 48-49

CHOUX PASTRY
½ cup butter or margarine
½ teaspoon salt
1 cup all-purpose flour,
sifted before measuring
4 eggs

FILLING
2 cups heavy or whipping cream
2 tablespoons granulated sugar
1 teaspoon vanilla extract

FROSTING
2 cups sifted confectioners' sugar
¼ cup chocolate-flavored quick-milk mix

About 3 hours before serving: Preheat oven to 400° F.
1. In medium saucepan over high heat, bring 1 cup water and butter to boiling; reduce heat. Vigorously stir in salt and flour until mixture forms a ball and leaves sides of pan.
2. Remove from heat; beat in eggs, one at a time, beating until thoroughly blended and smooth after each addition.
3. On greased cookie sheets, 2 inches apart, drop mixture by heaping tablespoonfuls. Spread mixture with spatula to form éclairs 4 inches long and 1 inch wide. Or use a pastry bag with plain tube to press out each éclair. Bake 40 minutes until puffed and golden. Remove éclairs to rack.

Just before serving: Prepare filling and frosting. In large bowl, beat cream with sugar and vanilla until stiff. Make lengthwise slit in the side of each cooled éclair; fill with cream; refrigerate.

In small bowl, combine confectioners' sugar and quick-milk mix; add 3½ tablespoons water and mix until smooth. Use to frost tops of éclairs. Makes 12 to 16 éclairs.

CREAM PUFFS: Make Choux Pastry as above. Drop mixture by tablespoonfuls, 3 inches apart, on greased cookie sheets; with back of spoon, shape each into mound that points up in the center. Bake as above for 50 minutes or until puffs are high and golden. Remove to rack to cool.

Slice tops off cream puffs and fill with whipped-cream filling (above) or ice cream. Replace tops and sprinkle with confectioners' sugar; serve with hot chocolate or butterscotch sauce. Makes 16 cream puffs or 8 servings.

ELEGANT CREAM-PUFF CAKE
pictured between pages 48-49

Choux Pastry (page 29)
⅓ cup semisweet-chocolate pieces
½ 11¼-ounce package
soft coconut macaroons (9)
3 envelopes unflavored gelatin
3 3¼-ounce packages
vanilla pudding-and-pie filling
1 tablespoon almond extract
7 cups heavy or whipping cream
1 cup confectioners' sugar
8 candied whole cherries

Day before: Preheat oven to 400° F. Grease and flour cookie sheet; on it, using an inverted 8-inch plate as guide, with knife, trace a circle. Prepare Choux Pastry as in steps 1 and 2 in Chocolate Eclairs.

Onto cookie sheet, just inside the 8-inch circle, by rounded serving tablespoonfuls, drop Choux Pastry, forming a ring. Bake 40 minutes without peeking (ring will be puffed, high and golden). Turn off oven heat and allow puff ring to rest in oven 15 minutes. Then, with spatula, remove it to rack; cool away from draft.

Prepare another batch of Choux Pastry and bake second ring the same way.

While second ring bakes, remove cooled ring from rack. With sharp knife, split it in half, crosswise; with spoon, remove interior, leaving a hollow ring shell. Dry out both halves on racks at room temperature, for 3 hours. Repeat with second cooled ring. In plastic wrap, wrap each cooled ring, top and bottom together.

In double boiler, over hot, *not boiling*, water, melt chocolate. On shallow pan, lay macaroons side by side. Brush with melted chocolate. Set in freezer 5 minutes, or until chocolate hardens, then cut macaroons in half; cover and set aside.

Early in day: Sprinkle 1 envelope of the gelatin over ¼ cup cold water; set over hot water, stirring until dissolved; cool slightly.

In large saucepan, prepare packages of pudding as label directs, but reduce milk to 4½ cups instead of the 6 called for; stir in almond extract and cooled gelatin. Turn into large bowl; place waxed paper directly on surface of pudding; cool.

In large bowl, whip 3 cups of the heavy cream; gradually fold it into cooled pudding. Set aside.

Unwrap cream-puff rings. Place one ring on 12-inch cake plate; lift off top; set aside. Fill bottom with half of filling; replace top. Place bottom of second ring (refrigerate top for use another day) on another plate; fill with remaining filling. Refrigerate filled rings.

Soften another envelope of gelatin in ¼ cup cold water; set over hot water, stirring until dissolved; cool slightly.

In medium bowl, beat 2 cups of the heavy cream with ½ cup confectioners' sugar until fairly stiff. Add cooled gelatin, beating until stiff. Make another batch of cream with remaining envelope of gelatin, 2 cups of cream and ½ cup confectioners' sugar.

Remove ring on 12-inch cake plate from refrigerator; frost entire ring with one batch of the whipped cream. Place second ring on top of frosted ring; cover all with second batch of whipped cream so that layers are hidden. Garnish with macaroons and cherries as pictured; chill. With warmed knife, cut into wedges to serve. Makes 20 servings.

ALMOND CREAM-PUFF RING

Choux Pastry (page 29)
1 3¾-ounce package
instant vanilla-pudding mix
1 cup heavy or whipping cream, whipped
1 teaspoon almond extract
½ cup semisweet-chocolate pieces
1 tablespoon butter or margarine
1½ teaspoons milk
1½ teaspoons light corn syrup

Early in day: Prepare Choux Pastry for cream-puff ring as in steps 1 and 2 in Chocolate Eclairs.

Preheat oven to 400° F. On greased, lightly floured cookie sheet, using an inverted 7-inch plate as a guide, with knife or finger, trace a circle. Drop heaping measuring tablespoonfuls of dough just inside the circle to form ring. Bake 40 minutes, without peeking, until golden and firm. Turn off oven heat and allow puff ring to remain in oven for 15 minutes. With spatula, remove ring to rack; let stand, away from draft, until completely cool.

With sharp knife, cut ring in half horizontally; with spoon, remove soft interior; discard, leaving a hollow ring shell.

In medium bowl, prepare instant vanilla-pudding mix as label directs, but use only 1¼ cups milk; gradually fold in whipped cream and almond extract.

Place bottom puff shell on cake platter. Fill with cream mixture; set top shell in place. Refrigerate.

In double boiler, over hot, *not boiling*, water, melt semisweet-chocolate pieces with butter, milk and corn syrup, stirring occasionally, until smooth. Spread chocolate mixture on top of ring. Refrigerate. Makes 10 servings.

APRI-APPLESAUCE

Early in day: Wash ½ pound dried apricots; place in saucepan with water to cover; simmer 45 minutes or until tender; drain.

In medium bowl, combine apricots with 2 tablespoons granulated sugar, two 15-ounce jars applesauce, ½ teaspoon ground ginger, 1 teaspoon vanilla extract, ¼ teaspoon nutmeg and 1 teaspoon cinnamon. Cover; refrigerate until serving time. Makes 4 to 6 servings.

DANISH PORCUPINE APPLES

¾ cup granulated sugar
2 tablespoons lemon juice
3 large cooking apples,
peeled, halved and cored
½ cup slivered toasted almonds
Custard Sauce (page 124)

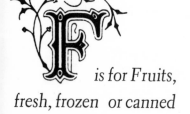

is for Fruits,
fresh, frozen or canned

Early in day: In large skillet, bring 2½ cups water, sugar and lemon juice to boiling. Add apples; cover; simmer, turning once, until tender. On deep serving platter, arrange apple halves, cut side down. Boil syrup in which apples cooked until it's reduced to 2 cups.

Tuck some of slivered almonds into rounded side of each apple half, to resemble porcupine. Pour on syrup; cool; refrigerate.

Serve with Custard Sauce. Makes 6 servings.

LAYERED APPLESAUCE

½ cup butter or margarine
2 cups uncooked quick rolled oats
2 tablespoons granulated sugar
1 16-ounce can applesauce, chilled
whipped cream, dessert topping
or Vanilla Sauce (page 125)

About ½ hour before serving: In medium skillet over medium heat, melt butter; add rolled oats; cook, stirring constantly, until golden. Stir in granulated sugar.

In each of 6 sherbet glasses, place about 2 heaping tablespoons of the applesauce. Top with about 3 heaping tablespoons of the rolled-oat mixture. Serve at once, with desired topping. Makes 6 servings.

APPLESAUCE SUPREME

1 25-ounce jar applesauce,
chilled (2¾ cups)
½ teaspoon nutmeg
1 2-ounce package whipped-topping mix
½ teaspoon almond extract
1½ cups fresh raspberries

About 20 minutes before serving: Into applesauce, stir nutmeg until well mixed; spoon into 6 sherbet dishes.

Prepare whipped-topping mix as label directs, using almond instead of vanilla extract. Spoon generous mounds of whipped topping over applesauce. Top each dessert with some of fresh raspberries. Makes 6 servings.

GLAZED APPLE FLAN

1 cup all-purpose flour
granulated sugar
½ cup butter or margarine
2 egg yolks, slightly beaten
12 apple slices
1 25-ounce jar applesauce
¼ teaspoon cinnamon
½ cup sour cream
3 tablespoons packed light
brown sugar

About 2 hours before serving: Preheat oven to 375° F. In large bowl, combine flour and ½ cup sugar. With pastry blender or 2 knives used scissor-fashion, cut in butter until mixture resembles coarse crumbs. Blend in egg yolks. Knead lightly to form smooth ball. Divide dough evenly into 6 balls; cover and refrigerate for ½ hour.

In each of six 4-inch flan pans, place one of the balls of dough. With fingers, press dough evenly to cover sides and bottom of pans; prick pastry with fork. Bake 15 minutes. Cool in pans on rack.

Meanwhile, in small saucepan, combine apple slices, ½ cup water and 2 tablespoons granulated sugar; cook over low heat until barely tender, about 5 minutes; drain on paper towels. Combine applesauce and cinnamon; half fill flan pans; top with a layer of sour cream, then remaining applesauce. Sprinkle with brown sugar; garnish each flan with 2 apple slices. Broil under medium heat 3 minutes, or until sugar caramelizes; cool. Remove from pans. Makes 6 servings.

HEAVENLY ORANGES

3 large seedless oranges
3 egg yolks
¼ cup granulated sugar
10 tablespoons orange juice
½ cup heavy or whipping cream
angel-food cake or ladyfingers (optional)

Early in day: With fine grater, grate peel from 1 orange; set aside. Peel and section all 3 oranges; place in serving dish; chill.

In bowl, beat egg yolks until light; gradually add sugar, then orange peel and juice. Cook in double boiler, over boiling water, beating constantly with rotary beater, until foamy, about 4 minutes. Cool; refrigerate.

About 10 minutes before serving: Beat cream until stiff; fold into orange sauce. Pour over orange sections and serve at once with angel-food cake or ladyfingers if desired. Makes 4 servings.

AMBROSIA

Several hours before serving: Slice 6 to 8 peeled oranges. In serving dish or sherbet glasses, arrange orange slices in layers with *confectioners' sugar* and *grated fresh, flaked* or *fine grated coconut.* Refrigerate until well chilled. Makes 6 to 8 servings.

⋖ DELUXE STYLE: Add *2 tablespoons grated orange peel* to *½ cup heavy cream;* chill. Whip cream until it forms soft mounds; stir in *3 tablespoons granulated sugar.* Pass with Ambrosia.

⋖ AMBROSIA SHELLS: Buy the biggest oranges you can find. Cut slice from top of each; then hollow out. Fill with the traditional ambrosia mixture, or *orange sections, canned crushed pineapple* and *flaked coconut.* Garnish each with a *tiny bunch of grapes.*

⋖ FRUIT-FILLED ORANGE SHELLS: Refill orange shells, made as in Ambrosia Shells, with orange sections tossed with *halved strawberries* and *bias slices of banana.* Serve, sprinkled with Lemon Sauce (page 124) . For some added crunch, mix *canned, slivered toasted almonds* with the fruit.

⋖ SOUTHERN AMBROSIA: At serving time, alternate layers of *Custard Sauce De Luxe* (page 124) , *well-drained orange sections* and *flaked canned or fresh coconut* in one large dish or in individual dishes. Makes 6 to 8 servings.

COOL RASPBERRY FONDUE
pictured between pages 48-49

½ pint fresh raspberries or 2 10-ounce packages
frozen raspberries, thawed
2 tablespoons granulated sugar
1 8-ounce package cream cheese, softened
½ pint strawberries
½ honeydew melon
½ pineapple
2 pears
lemon juice

About 1 hour before serving: In covered electric-blender container, thoroughly blend fresh raspberries with sugar. (Or blend well-drained, thawed, frozen berries.) Into small bowl, push raspberries through medium sieve, straining out seeds, but forcing pulp through.

In medium bowl, with electric mixer, beat cream cheese until smooth; gradually beat in raspberry pulp until well mixed and smooth. Refrigerate.

Wash strawberries; cut melon into balls; cut pineapple into strips; cut pears into thin wedges and dip in lemon juice. Arrange fruit on serving platter around bowl of the raspberry-cheese mixture. Using cocktail forks, dip fruit into mixture. Makes 6 servings.

GOLDEN FONDUE: *Prepare one 3-ounce package egg-custard mix as label directs for pudding, but use only 1⅓ cups milk; chill until slightly thickened. Stir until smooth; blend in 1 cup frozen whipped topping, thawed, and ½ teaspoon nutmeg. Cover surface with waxed paper; refrigerate. Serve in bowl surrounded with fresh fruit on platter as above.*

MINTED GRAPES

1 bunch seedless grapes
½ cup honey
2 tablespoons lime juice
2 tablespoons finely chopped mint

Several hours before serving: Wash and stem enough grapes to fill 4 parfait or sherbet glasses.

In medium bowl, stir together honey, lime juice and mint. Refrigerate grapes in this mixture until ready to serve, then spoon into glasses. Makes 4 servings.

HONEYDEW CRESCENTS

1 3-ounce package lime-flavor gelatin
1 medium honeydew melon
½ cup seedless green grapes
½ cup purple grapes
1 small pear
2 tablespoons frozen orange-juice concentrate

Early in day: In small bowl, dissolve gelatin in 1 cup boiling water. Chill until slightly thickened. Meanwhile, cut rind from honeydew melon. Cut thin slice from bottom so it will stand upright. Cut large slice from top. Remove seeds and pulp. Stand melon in deep bowl.

Cut green grapes in half. Cut purple grapes in half and remove seeds. Cut pear into bite-size pieces. In medium bowl, toss grapes and pear with orange-juice concentrate.

Brush outside of melon with 3 tablespoons of thickened gelatin; add remaining gelatin to fruit mixture. Put fruit mixture into melon cavity. Refrigerate 4 hours or until gelatin is firm.

To serve: Cut melon crosswise into 3 slices; cut each slice in half. Makes 6 servings.

SACRAMENTO FRUIT BOWL

1½ cups granulated sugar
3 tablespoons lemon juice
2 tablespoons anise seed
½ teaspoon salt
1 each: small pineapple, honeydew melon
and cantaloupe, peeled and cut
in bite-size chunks
2 oranges, peeled, sectioned
2 each: nectarines (or 4 apricots)
and purple plums, sliced in wedges
1 cup seedless grapes
1 lime, sliced

Early in day: In medium saucepan, combine 2 cups water with sugar, lemon juice, anise seed and salt. Cook over medium heat 15 minutes until mixture reaches light syrup consistency; chill.

In large bowl or other container, combine cut-up fruits with grapes and lime slices. Pour chilled syrup through strainer over fruits. Refrigerate, stirring occasionally. Makes 10 to 12 servings.

COUPE ESPAÑOL

1 orange
⅓ cup heavy or whipping cream
1 pear and 1 banana
½ pint orange sherbet

About 1 hour before serving: With knife, remove a thin layer of peel from orange; cut a few pieces of this peel into lengthwise strips, as narrow as possible. Whip cream; refrigerate.

At serving time: Into 4 sherbet glasses, dice cored, peeled pear. Top with diced, peeled banana. Spoon a little whipped cream over each glass of fruit, then top with spoonful of sherbet. Sprinkle bit of slivered orange peel over each. Serve at once. Makes 4 servings.

TWO-DIP DESSERT FONDUE

2 medium pears
2 medium apples
ascorbic-acid mixture for fruit
4 plain doughnuts, cut in chunks
1 7½-ounce package thick ring pretzels
1 6-ounce can pecans, finely chopped
½ cup butter or margarine
2 cups light cream
1½ cups packed light brown sugar
½ cup granulated sugar
⅛ teaspoon salt
⅛ teaspoon nutmeg
⅛ teaspoon cinnamon

About 45 minutes before serving: Cut pears and apples into bite-size pieces; toss in ascorbic-acid mixture as label directs to prevent them from turning brown. Arrange fruits, doughnuts and pretzels on platter. Place chopped pecans in small bowl.

In fondue pot, on range over medium heat, bring butter, cream, sugars and spices to boiling.* Do not stir. Boil about 15 minutes until mixture sheets when dropped from a spoon. Use pastry brush dipped in hot water to brush sugar crystals away from sides of pot occasionally.

At serving time: Place fondue pot on stand over low heat. Guests dip fruits, doughnuts and pretzels into hot caramel, then into chopped pecans. (Provide fondue forks for dipping fruits and doughnuts.) Makes 8 to 10 dessert servings.

*If using an electric fondue set, prepare hot caramel sauce directly on fondue base, using high-heat setting; reduce heat to low to serve.

STREUSEL PEAR FLAN

1½ cups all-purpose flour
¼ teaspoon salt
¼ cup granulated sugar
½ cup butter or margarine
2 egg yolks
2 29-ounce cans pear halves, drained
1 cup fresh white bread crumbs
¼ cup packed dark brown sugar
2 tablespoons chopped candied orange peel
4 candied cherries, halved
2 tablespoons apricot preserves

Several hours before serving: Into mixing bowl, sift flour, salt, sugar. With pastry blender, cut in butter until mixture resembles coarse crumbs. Blend in egg yolks and 1 tablespoon cold water. Roll out dough on well-floured waxed paper or pastry cloth to approximately a 10-inch circle to fit into greased fluted 9-inch flan pan with removable bottom. Trim pastry edges.

Preheat oven to 400° F. Set aside 8 pear halves; chop up remainder to make 2½ cups; spread over flan bottom. Mix together bread crumbs, sugar and peel. Sprinkle over chopped pears. Arrange pear halves on top of flan with cherry halves in between. Place flan on cookie sheet; bake 1 hour. While still hot, brush pears with warm apricot preserves. Cool; refrigerate. Nice served cold with sour cream. Makes 8 to 10 servings.

SPICED FRUIT COMPOTE

2 large oranges, peeled
1 30-ounce can apricots, drained
2 29-ounce cans pear halves, drained
1½ cups orange juice
¼ cup granulated sugar
2 or 3 short cinnamon sticks
12 whole cloves
½ teaspoon salt
¼ teaspoon ginger

Early in day: Into large bowl, cut oranges into large pieces. Add apricots and pear halves. In saucepan, simmer orange juice, sugar, cinnamon sticks, cloves, salt and ginger 5 minutes; pour over fruit. Cover; refrigerate 2 hours. Makes 8 servings.

CARIBBEAN PINEAPPLE SPEARS

½ cup light corn syrup
¼ cup lemon juice
½ teaspoon rum extract
1 pineapple
fresh mint sprigs

Early in day: In deep bowl, combine syrup, juice and rum extract.
Remove top and slice bottom from pineapple, then slice it lengthwise
into quarters. Slice each quarter into fourths, making 16 spears in all.
Cut off outer rind; remove core and eyes. Marinate spears in syrup mixture in refrigerator for several hours, turning occasionally.
At serving time: Arrange pineapple spears upright in glass bowl. Garnish with mint sprigs. Makes 4 to 6 servings.

SUMMERTIME PINEAPPLE

Several hours before serving: Prepare one or both pineapples. For the
tall version, stand *a large pineapple* on wooden board; grasp by crown;
with sharp knife, cut off rind, following the curve of the fruit. Cut slice
from bottom. With pointed knife, remove eyes, then cut lengthwise
through crown into 6 wedges. Stand up in bowl, with *1 or 2 pints
strawberries* in between; refrigerate. Makes 6 servings.
For the short version, cut *a large pineapple* into halves, lengthwise
through crown. With sharp knife, hollow out one half; cut fruit into
1-inch cubes; return to pineapple shell. Cut rind off other half; cut out
eyes, then cut crosswise into ¼-inch slices; cut core from each slice.
Arrange slices, overlapping, on top of filled pineapple shell; garnish
with *1 pint strawberries*; refrigerate. Makes 6 servings.

QUICK CRÈME BRÛLÉE

1 10-ounce package frozen peaches,
or 1 10-ounce package
frozen raspberries, thawed
½ cup sour cream
¼ cup packed brown sugar

About 5 minutes before serving: In 6-inch shallow baking dish, place
well-drained fruit; spread with sour cream. Sift brown sugar over cream.
Preheat broiler if manufacturer directs. Broil 3 inches from heat until
sugar caramelizes, about 1 or 2 minutes. Serve at once. Makes 2 servings.

BAKED FRUIT CUP

1 8-ounce can fruit cocktail, drained
1 medium banana, diced
½ teaspoon grated lemon peel
¼ cup all-purpose flour
¼ cup packed brown sugar
¼ teaspoon cinnamon
3 tablespoons butter or margarine

About 1 hour before serving: Preheat oven to 400° F. Mix fruit cocktail with banana and lemon peel; arrange in 4 custard cups. With fork, mix flour, brown sugar, cinnamon and butter until crumbly; sprinkle over fruit. Bake 20 minutes or until top is lightly browned. Serve warm or cold, with light cream. Makes 4 servings.

PRUNE SNOW

Early in day: In bowl, combine 1¾ cups sieved, cooked prunes, 1 teaspoon grated lemon peel, 2 tablespoons lemon juice, and ⅛ teaspoon cinnamon. In another bowl, with rotary beater, beat 2 egg whites with 3 tablespoons granulated sugar until stiff. Fold into prune mixture. Serve with Custard Sauce (page 124), or whipped cream. Makes 6 servings.

CHERRIES JUBILEE

1½ quarts vanilla ice cream
¾ cup currant jelly
1 29-ounce can pitted Bing cherries, drained
½ cup brandy

About 2 hours before serving: Make 8 large ice-cream balls and freeze on cookie sheet. Refrigerate 8 serving dishes.

At serving time: Place ice cream in dishes and bring to table. In chafing dish over direct heat, melt currant jelly, stirring constantly; add cherries and heat slowly until simmering. Pour brandy into center of fruit. (Do not stir.) Let brandy heat, undisturbed; when warmed, light with match. Spoon flaming fruit over ice cream. Makes 8 servings.

⊸§ PEACHES JUBILEE: Use one 29-ounce can sliced peaches instead of cherries.

⊸§ STRAWBERRIES JUBILEE: Use two 10-ounce packages frozen whole strawberries instead of cherries.

PEAR ELEGANCE

8 canned pear halves, drained
¼ cup cocoa
1 egg yolk
½ cup heavy or whipping cream
¼ cup confectioners' sugar
1½ teaspoons brandy

Night before: In center cavity of each of 4 pear halves, place 1 table-spoon of the cocoa. Top each filled half with inverted unfilled half, making "whole" pear; refrigerate.

Just before serving: In small bowl, beat egg yolk; fold into cream, whipped with confectioners' sugar and brandy. In 4 dessert dishes, arrange one "whole" pear; top with whipped cream. Makes 4 servings.

BANANA-COCONUT ROLLS

About ½ hour before serving: Preheat oven to 375° F. Halve *4 peeled, firm bananas crosswise; place in greased 10" by 6" pan. Brush with 2 tablespoons melted butter or margarine and 2 tablespoons lemon juice or lime juice; sprinkle with ½ cup flaked coconut.* Bake 15 to 20 minutes or until easily pierced with fork.

Serve warm, with *cream.* Makes 4 servings.

TWO-BERRY AMBROSIA

1 10-ounce package frozen raspberries
1 10-ounce package frozen strawberries
1 pound seedless grapes
or ½ pound pitted halved Malaga grapes
½ to 1 pint sour cream
2 cups flaked coconut
confectioners' sugar (optional)

Just before serving: When berries are just thawed, in large bowl, combine them with grapes, sour cream and coconut (save some cream and coconut for garnish). Add sugar if mixture isn't sweet enough; toss together lightly.

Serve, buffet style, in decorative bowl, topped with small blobs of sour cream and sprinkling of coconut; or spoon into sherbet glasses. Makes 10 servings.

LEMON-ORANGE FRUIT SHIMMER
pictured between pages 48-49

1 11-ounce can mandarin-orange sections
1 3-ounce package lemon-flavor gelatin

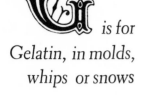

is for Gelatin, in molds, whips or snows

Early in day: Into 2-cup measure, drain juice from mandarin-orange sections. To juice, add enough boiling water to make 2 cups liquid. In small bowl, combine lemon gelatin with hot liquid; stir until gelatin is completely dissolved.

Fill 4 parfait glasses, small goblets or wine glasses, ⅓ full of dissolved gelatin. Using ⅓ of the drained mandarin-orange sections, spoon some into each glass. Refrigerate glasses until gelatin mixture is just set, but not quite firm. (Refrigerate remaining orange sections and gelatin as well.)

To mixture in glasses, using half of the remaining gelatin and fruit, add another layer of gelatin, then another of fruit. Refrigerate until just set but not firm.

Top with remaining gelatin and fruit; refrigerate until serving time. If desired, serve topped with ice cream, whipped cream, sour cream or dessert topping. Makes 4 servings.

LIME-GRAPE: In small saucepan, bring *2 cups water** to boiling; remove from heat. Add *one 3-ounce package lime-flavor gelatin* and *1 tablespoon lime juice;* stir until gelatin is completely dissolved. Using *⅔ cup whole* or *halved seedless grapes* as fruit, proceed as above, layering and chilling the lime gelatin and grapes.

MARASCHINO CHERRY: In small saucepan, bring *2 cups water* to boiling; remove from heat. Add *one 3-ounce package cherry-flavor gelatin* and *1 teaspoon lemon juice;* stir until gelatin is completely dissolved. Using *½ cup maraschino cherries* as fruit, proceed as above, layering and chilling cherry gelatin and maraschino cherries.

CHERRY-PINEAPPLE: Into 2-cup measure, drain juice from *one 13½-ounce can pineapple chunks;* to the juice, add enough *boiling water* to make 2 cups liquid. In small bowl, combine *one 3-ounce package cherry-flavor gelatin* and the hot liquid; stir until gelatin is completely dissolved. Using drained pineapple chunks, proceed as above, layering and chilling cherry gelatin and pineapple.

* ½ cup sherry may replace ½ cup water.

PINEAPPLE-SNOW PUDDING

3½ cups canned pineapple juice
3 envelopes unflavored gelatin
6 tablespoons granulated sugar
2 teaspoons grated lemon peel
¼ cup lemon juice
⅛ teaspoon salt
1½ cups heavy or whipping cream
1¼ cups flaked coconut
2 cups halved strawberries
(or 1 10-ounce package frozen strawberries,
thawed and drained)
4 canned pineapple slices, quartered

Day before or early in day: In small bowl, combine 1 cup of the pineapple juice, gelatin and sugar; let stand 5 minutes. Set bowl in pan of boiling water and stir until gelatin is dissolved.

In large bowl, combine remaining 2½ cups pineapple juice, lemon peel and juice and salt. Stir in gelatin mixture. Refrigerate until slightly thicker than unbeaten egg white.

Whip cream until soft peaks form. Whip gelatin mixture until fluffy. Gently fold gelatin and ¾ cup of the coconut into whipped cream. Pour into 2-quart mold; refrigerate.

Just before serving: Unmold pudding onto large platter; arrange strawberries and pineapple pieces around mold, reserving a few strawberries. Sprinkle mold and fruit with remaining coconut; garnish with reserved berries. Makes 12 servings.

COFFEE JELLY

2 envelopes unflavored gelatin
⅔ cup granulated sugar
¼ teaspoon salt
2 cups hot coffee
2 teaspoons lemon juice

Early in day: In medium bowl, over 1 cup cold water, sprinkle gelatin to soften. Add sugar, salt, hot coffee; stir until gelatin dissolves; stir in lemon juice. Pour into 4-cup mold or six ⅔-cup individual molds. Refrigerate until set.

To serve: Unmold onto serving plate. Nice topped with cream, whipped cream, Custard Sauce (page 124), sliced bananas or peaches. Makes 6 servings.

NECTARINE-CHEESE MOLD

¾ cup all-purpose flour
⅓ cup butter or margarine, softened
granulated sugar
2 egg yolks
1 tablespoon grated lemon peel
½ cup milk
1 envelope unflavored gelatin
⅛ teaspoon salt
1 8-ounce package cream cheese, softened
2 tablespoons grated orange peel
1 egg white
1 3-ounce package lemon-
flavor gelatin
4 nectarines, cut in thick slices

Early in day: Preheat oven to 400° F. In medium bowl, combine flour, butter, 2 tablespoons sugar, 1 of the egg yolks and lemon peel. With pastry blender or 2 knives used scissor-fashion, cut mixture into pieces the size of peas. With hands, shape into ball; spread firmly in bottom (not on sides) of 10-inch springform pan. Bake 8 to 10 minutes or until light golden brown; cool.

In double boiler, beat remaining egg yolk slightly, then beat in milk until well mixed. Add unflavored gelatin, ⅓ cup granulated sugar and salt; cook over hot, *not boiling*, water, stirring constantly, until gelatin is dissolved and mixture slightly thickened, about 10 minutes. Remove from heat.

In small bowl, with electric mixer at medium speed, beat cream cheese and orange peel until smooth. Gradually beat in gelatin mixture until well blended. Wash beaters.

In another small bowl, with electric mixer at high speed, beat egg white until soft peaks form. Fold into cheese mixture. Cool in refrigerator 10 minutes or until mixture mounds slightly. Pour evenly onto crust; chill ½ hour.

In small bowl, dissolve lemon gelatin in ¾ cup boiling water; stir in ¾ cup cold water; cool until lukewarm. Arrange nectarine slices on cheese mixture in overlapping circles. Place mold in refrigerator; carefully pour gelatin over nectarines; chill until firm, at least 3 hours.

To serve: Dip spatula in hot water to loosen edge of mold from pan; carefully remove sides of springform pan. Makes 8 to 10 servings.

◦§ PEACH-CHEESE MOLD: Use 3 or 4 peaches, cut in thick slices, instead of nectarines in above recipe.

FRUIT FANTASY
pictured between pages 48–49

2 3-ounce packages
orange-pineapple-flavor gelatin
boiling water
⅔ cup lemon-flavor carbonated beverage
⅔ cup Chablis or sauterne
ice cubes
4 or 5 thin peach slices,
canned, fresh, or thawed frozen
seedless grapes

Early in day before serving: Get out 2-quart china soufflé dish, or dish of the same capacity with flat bottom and straight sides.

In bowl, combine gelatin with 1½ cups of boiling water; stir until gelatin is completely dissolved. Add lemon-flavor carbonated beverage and Chablis; stir until well blended.

Partially fill large bowl with ice cubes. Place bowl of gelatin in ice cubes; stir constantly until gelatin just mounds when dropped from a spoon.

Remove bowl from ice. Pour 2 cups of the gelatin mixture into soufflé dish; arrange peach slices and ⅓ cup seedless grapes in dish as pictured.

Carefully spoon remaining gelatin mixture over first gelatin layer. Refrigerate until firm.

Just before serving: Into bowl of hot water, up to ½ inch of its top, lower soufflé dish for 1 or 2 minutes. Remove at once and run long spatula around edge, being sure it goes all the way to bottom of dish so gelatin is completely loosened.

Unmold onto cake plate. Garnish with small bunches of seedless grapes. Makes 6 servings.

TWO-LAYER: Prepare gelatin as above, but refrigerate only about 40 minutes until almost firm. In bowl, with fork, beat *four 3-ounce packages cream cheese,* at room temperature, with *¼ teaspoon nutmeg, dash cinnamon* and *6 tablespoons milk* until mixture is smooth and creamy; spoon evenly over gelatin layer; clean any spills from sides of dish; refrigerate. Prepare *2 more 3-ounce packages orange-pineapple flavor gelatin* as above, using another *⅔ cup lemon-flavor carbonated beverage* and *⅔ cup Chablis;* chill just until gelatin mixture mounds when dropped from spoon. Spoon over cream-cheese layer; refrigerate overnight. Loosen gelatin, unmold and garnish as above. Makes 12 servings.

JIFFY JELLIED FRUIT

1 3-ounce package
favorite fruit-flavor gelatin
1 cup boiling water
½ cup fruit juice or cold water
1 tablespoon lemon juice
10-ounce package frozen sliced strawberries,
raspberries, or sliced peaches, unthawed
1 cup seedless grapes

About 1 hour before serving: In medium bowl, dissolve gelatin in boiling water; stir in fruit juice or cold water and remaining ingredients. Refrigerate, stirring occasionally, until frozen fruit thaws and gelatin sets—about ½ hour for soft jelly, or 1 hour for firm jelly. Spoon into 6 sherbet glasses. Top with Custard Sauce (page 124) or whipped dessert topping, if desired. Makes 6 servings.

~§ DATE-NUT: Prepare jelly as above, but instead of seedless grapes, substitute *½ cup chopped walnuts or pecans and ½ cup chopped, pitted dates.*

~§ PINE-MALLOW: Prepare jelly as above, substituting *one 8½-ounce can pineapple tidbits,* undrained, for ½ cup fruit juice or cold water and seedless grapes. When gelatin begins to thicken, fold in *16 miniature marshmallows or 4 large marshmallows,* quartered; refrigerate until set.

ORANGE-JELLY BAGATELLE

1 3-ounce package orange-flavor gelatin
½ cup boiling water
1 16-ounce can applesauce (2 cups)
grated orange peel
nutmeg
whipped dessert topping

Early in day: In bowl, stir gelatin into water until completely dissolved. Add applesauce, 2 teaspoons orange peel and ⅛ teaspoon nutmeg. Pour into 9″ by 5″ loaf pan; refrigerate until set.

To serve: Cut jelly into 1-inch squares; heap into 4 sherbet glasses. Top with whipped topping; sprinkle with grated orange peel and nutmeg. Makes 4 servings.

HEAVENLY ORANGE WHIP

4 to 5 medium oranges
4 egg yolks
2½ cups orange juice
2 envelopes unflavored gelatin
¾ cup granulated sugar
⅛ teaspoon salt
3 tablespoons lemon juice
2 cups heavy or whipping cream

Day before or early in day: Grate 1 of the oranges; reserve grated peel and remove sections. Then peel and section remaining oranges. Cut enough sections in half to make 1½ cups; set aside. Refrigerate any extra orange sections to use for garnish.

In medium saucepan, with wire whisk or rotary beater, beat egg yolks slightly, then beat in 1 cup of the orange juice until well blended. Stir in gelatin, sugar and salt. Cook mixture over medium heat, stirring constantly, until just boiling, or until gelatin and sugar are dissolved. Remove from heat. Stir in reserved orange peel, remaining 1½ cups orange juice and lemon juice.

Chill, stirring occasionally, until mixture mounds when dropped from spoon. Whip cream. Fold in reserved 1½ cups orange sections, then whipped cream. Pour into 8- to 10-cup mold. Chill several hours until set.

Just before serving: Unmold and garnish with extra orange sections if desired. Makes 10 to 12 servings.

RAINBOW WHIP

1 3-ounce package lemon-flavor gelatin
1 3-ounce package lime-flavor gelatin
1 3-ounce package strawberry-flavor gelatin
1 cup whipped-dessert topping

Early in day: In separate bowl, prepare each package of gelatin as label directs. Refrigerate bowls until gelatin mounds when dropped from spoon, then remove from refrigerator.

With electric mixer at high speed, beat lemon gelatin until fluffy; spoon into 6 to 8 sherbet glasses. Refrigerate until set, then top with whipped lime gelatin; refrigerate. When set, top with whipped strawberry gelatin; refrigerate.

To serve: Top with whipped-dessert topping. Makes 6 to 8 servings.

CRANBERRY SALAD-DESSERT MOLD

6 oranges
4 cups fresh cranberries, coarsely chopped
2 cups granulated sugar
4 3-ounce packages
strawberry-flavor gelatin
3 cups boiling water
1 tablespoon lemon juice
15 to 20 fresh whole cranberries

Early in day: Prepare the orange peel "mum" for garnish first. Slice top from one of oranges, about ¼ of the way down. With sharp knife, cut out all the orange sections; set aside. With kitchen scissors, carefully snip orange shell from cut edge down about ¾ of the way toward stem end; repeat this snipping at ¼-inch intervals, all the way around to form fringe. Cut top of each strip into point to form petals . Repeat with another orange. Wrap the two "mums" in foil or plastic wrap; refrigerate.

Peel 3 of the oranges. Cut oranges and reserved orange sections into pea-size pieces. In bowl, combine cut-up oranges with chopped cranberries and sugar. Mix until sugar dissolves.

In large bowl, dissolve strawberry-flavor gelatin in boiling water; add 3 cups cold water, lemon juice and cranberry-orange mixture. Refrigerate, stirring occasionally, until mixture thickens to egg-white consistency; pour into 3-quart bundt pan; refrigerate until firm.

About 20 minutes before serving: Set bundt pan, just up to rim, in warm water for 10 seconds. Lift from water; shake pan slightly to loosen gelatin from mold; unmold onto serving platter.

Using sharp knife, cut remaining orange into 5 crosswise slices; cut each orange slice in half and arrange around cranberry mold; top each half with 1 or 2 whole cranberries. Place orange-peel "mums," one inside other, in center of cranberry mold, as garnish. Makes 16 servings.

EASY RASPBERRY CREAM

Day before serving: In large saucepan over high heat, bring *3 cups water* to boiling. Turn heat to low; using large spoon, stir in *one 6-ounce package raspberry-flavor gelatin* until just dissolved. Quickly stir in *2 pints vanilla ice cream*, using spoon to cut ice cream into small pieces to hasten melting (mixture should be only lukewarm) . Pour into deep 2-quart mold. Chill. Unmold to serve. Makes 10 servings.

Cream-filled Chocolate Éclairs, **page** 29, a pastry-shop confection easily made at home

Cream-puff rings filled with almond cream make this Elegant Cream-Puff Cake, page 30

Cool Raspberry Fondue, page 35 — a delightful dip for many kinds of fruit

Fruit Fantasy, page 45, an easy dessert designed for a lazy day

Fruit Shimmer, page 42, a spectacular way to serve fruit, layered in your favorite gelatin dessert

Lime Cream Sherbet, page 57, cool and tangy, as refreshing as a summer breeze.
For a crisp treat to go with it, deep-fry a basketful of Rosettes, page 132

Big-Top Sundae page 63, an ice-cream delight for children and adults alike

There's rum mousse hiding in the heart of this handsome Raspberry Snowball, page 66

HARVEST NUT PUDDING

2 cups all-purpose flour,
sifted before measuring
¼ teaspoon baking soda
1½ teaspoons double-acting baking powder
¾ cup canned pumpkin
¼ cup buttermilk
½ cup shortening
1 teaspoon salt
1 teaspoon cinnamon
½ teaspoon ginger
½ teaspoon nutmeg
¼ cup granulated sugar
1 cup packed dark brown sugar
2 eggs
1 cup finely chopped Brazil nuts

About 3 hours before serving: Sift together flour, soda and baking powder. Mix pumpkin with buttermilk.

In large bowl, with electric mixer at medium speed, thoroughly mix shortening with salt, spices, sugars and eggs until creamy. Then, at low speed, beat in flour mixture alternately with pumpkin mixture, beating after each addition until smooth. Beat in nuts.

Turn batter into well greased 1½-quart mold; cover mold and prepare to steam as in steps 3 and 4 of Cranberry Steamed Pudding (page 51). Steam 2 hours. Let stand 5 minutes; remove from mold. Serve with Custard Sauce (page 124) or soft ice cream. Makes about 8 servings.

 *is for Holiday steamed puddings, aflame or with sauce*

SPICY OATMEAL PUDDING

1 cup all-purpose flour,
sifted before measuring
¾ cup granulated sugar
¾ teaspoon salt
1⅛ teaspoons baking soda
1 teaspoon cinnamon
1 cup rolled oats
¾ cup raisins
3 tablespoons melted shortening
1¼ cups buttermilk
1½ teaspoons vanilla extract
candied fruits
vanilla ice cream

About 2½ hours before serving:* Into large bowl, sift flour, sugar, salt, baking soda and cinnamon; stir in rolled oats and raisins.

Generously grease 2-quart steamed-pudding mold. Set aside.

In 2-cup measure, combine shortening, buttermilk and vanilla. Pour all at once into flour mixture; stir until well blended. Turn into prepared mold and prepare to steam as in steps 3 and 4 of Cranberry Steamed Pudding(opposite). Simmer 1½ hours or until cake tester inserted in center of pudding comes out clean.

Let pudding stand on rack 5 minutes, then unmold onto serving plate; surround with candied fruits and top with softened vanilla ice cream. Makes about 10 servings.

*To do ahead: Steam pudding as above; unmold; cool. Wrap cooled pudding in foil; refrigerate. To serve, heat foil-wrapped pudding in 325° F. oven for 1 hour or until hot; unwrap and serve as above.

TINY TIM'S PLUM PUDDING

3½ cups all-purpose flour,
sifted before measuring
2 cups packed brown sugar
¼ teaspoon each cinnamon, nutmeg,
ground cloves and ginger
1 teaspoon salt
2 cups ground suet
2 cups chopped raisins
2 cups currants
1 cup chopped dried figs
2 cups diced citron
1 teaspoon diced candied orange peel
1 teaspoon diced candied lemon peel
3 eggs, well beaten
1 cup orange juice
Hard Sauce(opposite) or ice cream

Several days ahead: In large bowl, mix flour, sugar, spices, salt, suet; stir in fruits and peels. Add eggs, 1 cup water and orange juice; mix well. Turn into greased 2- to 2½-quart tall mold; cover mold and prepare to steam as in steps 3 and 4 of Cranberry Steamed Pudding(opposite). Steam 5 hours. Let stand 5 minutes; remove from mold; cool. Wrap in foil; refrigerate.

About 2 hours before serving: Bake foil-wrapped pudding at 325° F. 2 hours or until hot. Or steam in mold 1 hour. Serve with Hard Sauce or ice-cream. Makes 20 servings.

CRANBERRY STEAMED PUDDING

3 eggs, beaten
3 cups cranberries, coarsely chopped
3 cups fine vanilla-wafer crumbs
1½ cups granulated sugar
½ cup blanched slivered almonds,
coarsely chopped
½ cup all-purpose flour
1 tablespoon double-acting baking powder
1 teaspoon cinnamon
¾ teaspoon salt
½ teaspoon ground cloves
¼ teaspoon ginger
¾ cup milk
¾ cup melted butter or margarine
Hard Sauce (below)

1. *About 4 hours before serving:* In large bowl, combine eggs and next 10 ingredients. Stir in milk and melted butter until well mixed.
2. Pour into well-greased, 3-quart ovenproof bowl or mold.
3. Cover tightly with greased foil; tie with string.
4. Place bowl on trivet in deep kettle. Add enough boiling water to come half way up sides of bowl.
5. Cover; simmer 3 hours 15 minutes, adding more boiling water if needed. Loosen and invert pudding onto platter; serve with Hard Sauce. Makes 12 servings.

HARD SAUCE

In small bowl, with electric mixer at medium speed, beat 2¼ *cups confectioners' sugar* and ¾ *cup butter or margarine,* softened, until fluffy. Beat in *5 tablespoons brandy.* Makes 2 cups.

CRANBERRY HOLIDAY PUDDING

3 cups cranberries
¾ cup light or dark raisins
2¼ cups all-purpose flour,
sifted before measuring
1 tablespoon baking soda
¾ cup light molasses
½ cup hot water
Hard Sauce (above)

*About 1½ hours before serving:** Rinse cranberries and raisins; drain; place in mixing bowl. Sift flour and baking soda over fruit. Add molasses and water; stir until well blended. Spoon into two 1-pound greased, lightly sugared coffee cans; prepare to steam as in steps 3 and 4 of Cranberry Steamed Pudding(page 51). Steam 1 hour 15 minutes or until done. Serve with Hard Sauce. Makes about 12 servings.

To do ahead: Make pudding several days ahead. Cool; remove from pans; wrap in foil and refrigerate. To serve, bake foil-wrapped pudding in 325° F. oven 45 minutes or until hot.

FLAMING PUDDING

Just before serving: Place hot *steamed pudding* on heatproof platter. For a large pudding, in a small saucepan, heat *½ cup brandy* until lukewarm; for individual puddings, heat *2 teaspoons brandy* for each pudding. Immediately pour brandy over and around hot pudding. Touch lighted match to brandy; carry to table, ablaze.

Or, soak *cubes of sugar* in *lemon extract;* place around pudding, or place one cube in top center of individual pudding; light with match.

GRANDMOTHER'S PLUM PUDDING

2 cups packaged dried bread crumbs
1 teaspoon cinnamon
¼ teaspoon ground cloves
1 teaspoon allspice
1 cup finely ground suet
¾ cup molasses
2 eggs
1½ cups milk
½ cup diced candied citron or mixed fruit
1 15-ounce package seedless raisins
1 tablespoon flour
Hard Sauce (page 51)

Early in day: In large bowl, combine crumbs, cinnamon, cloves, allspice, suet, molasses, eggs and milk, blending well after each addition. Toss together citron, raisins, flour; stir into batter.

Turn batter into top of well-greased 2-quart double boiler. Cover; cook over boiling water, adding more water as needed, for 5 hours. Run spatula around inside edge of pan and unmold pudding. Serve hot, with Hard Sauce. Makes 8 servings.

To do ahead: Make and steam pudding day before; refrigerate. To serve, reheat in double-boiler top about 1 hour.

SPICY APPLE MOLD

1½ cups all-purpose flour,
sifted before measuring
1 teaspoon baking soda
½ teaspoon each cinnamon, nutmeg
and ground cloves
¼ cup butter or margarine
1 cup granulated sugar
2 eggs, well beaten
3 large Rome Beauty apples,
peeled and shredded (2½ cups)
¾ cup apricot preserves
2 tablespoons light corn syrup
¼ cup seedless grapes, halved

About 2½ hours before serving: Grease 1½-quart heatproof bowl. Sift together flour, baking soda, spices. In large bowl, with electric mixer at medium speed, beat butter, sugar and eggs until smooth and light. Stir in apples and flour mixture until well blended. Turn into prepared bowl. Prepare to steam as in steps 3 and 4 of Cranberry Steamed Pudding (page 51). Simmer 2 hours. Cool on rack 5 minutes; unmold.

In small saucepan, combine apricot preserves and corn syrup; heat; add grapes; pour over Spicy Apple Mold. Makes 8 servings.

FRUIT-CAPPED STEAMED PUDDING

1 cup mixed dried fruits
3 tablespoons apricot preserves
½ cup butter or margarine
½ cup granulated sugar
2 eggs
1 cup self-rising flour
1 teaspoon grated lemon peel
1 teaspoon lemon juice
Custard Sauce (page 124)

About 3 hours before serving: In small bowl, cover fruits with water to soften for 1 hour. Drain; remove pits; chop half of fruit; set aside. Grease 1½-pint heatproof bowl; spread 2 tablespoons of the apricot preserves in bottom; on it, arrange some of unchopped fruit; spread remaining tablespoon of preserves halfway up sides of bowl; press remaining unchopped fruit into preserves.

In large bowl, with electric mixer at medium speed, beat butter until smooth; add sugar and beat until well blended. Beat in eggs, one at a time and continue beating until mixture is light and fluffy. Fold in flour with lemon peel and juice. Spoon half of the batter over fruit and preserves; cover with reserved chopped fruit; top with remaining batter. Prepare to steam as in steps 3 and 4 of Cranberry Steamed Pudding (page 51).

Simmer over medium heat for 1½ hours, adding more boiling water if necessary. Cool on rack 5 minutes. Remove foil; run a spatula gently around inside edge of bowl; unmold pudding onto serving plate; serve with Custard Sauce. Makes 6 servings.

MOCHA NUT PUDDING

1½ cups all-purpose flour,
sifted before measuring
¼ teaspoon salt
¼ teaspoon cream of tartar
⅛ teaspoon baking soda
2 1-ounce squares unsweetened chocolate
2 tablespoons butter or margarine
¾ cup packed brown sugar
2 eggs
⅓ cup milk
6 tablespoons finely chopped walnuts
2 teaspoons instant coffee
½ cup granulated sugar
½ teaspoon dark corn syrup

About 2½ hours before serving: Grease 1½ pint heatproof bowl. Sift together flour, salt, cream of tartar, baking soda.

In small saucepan over low heat, melt butter and chocolate. In large bowl, beat eggs until foamy; add brown sugar; beat until well blended. Blend in chocolate mixture; fold in flour mixture and 4 tablespoons of the walnuts alternately with milk until well blended. Pour into greased bowl; prepare to steam as in steps 3 and 4 of Cranberry Steamed Pudding (page 51).

Simmer 1 hour 15 minutes, adding more boiling water if needed. Cool on rack 5 minutes; remove foil. Run spatula around sides of pudding; unmold onto serving plate.

In saucepan, dissolve coffee and granulated sugar in 6 tablespoons water and corn syrup. Over medium heat, bring to boiling; boil until syrupy, stirring occasionally; remove from heat; quickly stir in remaining walnuts; pour over pudding. Makes 8 servings.

CRANBERRY PUDDING MOLD

½ cup butter or margarine
1 cup granulated sugar
2 eggs
about 3 cups cake flour,
sifted before measuring
3½ teaspoons double-acting baking powder
⅛ teaspoon salt
¾ cup milk
1½ cups whole cranberries
Hard Sauce (page 51) or light cream

About 2 hours before serving: Thoroughly grease and flour 1½-quart tube mold. In large bowl, with electric mixer at medium speed, beat butter until creamy. Gradually add sugar while beating, until mixture is light and fluffy. Add eggs; beat well.

Sift together 2¾ cups of the flour, baking powder and salt. With mixer at low speed, beat flour and milk alternately into egg mixture, starting and ending with flour. Coat cranberries with 3 tablespoons of the flour; fold into batter. Spoon into mold; prepare to steam as in steps 3 and 4 of Cranberry Steamed Pudding (page 51). Cover; simmer 1 hour 10 minutes or until done, adding more boiling water if needed.

Uncover mold and cool on rack ½ hour; with long spatula, carefully loosen pudding from sides; unmold. Cut pudding into fourths lengthwise with pie server; place each wedge on plate and cut into 3 equal portions. Serve with Hard Sauce or cream. Makes 12 servings.

OVEN-STEAMED PRUNE PUDDING

1½ cups cooked dried prunes
plus cooking liquid
2 cups all-purpose flour,
sifted before measuring
3 teaspoons double-acting baking powder
1 teaspoon salt
1 teaspoon cinnamon
½ teaspoon allspice
¼ teaspoon nutmeg
1 cup packed brown sugar
⅓ cup shortening
1 egg
½ cup diced candied fruits
½ cup chopped walnuts

About 2 hours before serving: Preheat oven to 375° F. Drain prunes, reserving ¾ cup liquid. Pit prunes, then chop. Sift together flour, baking powder, salt and spices. In bowl, with electric mixer at medium speed, cream sugar and shortening; add egg; beat until light and fluffy. At low speed, beat in flour mixture alternately with prune liquid just until mixed. Stir in prunes, candied fruits and nuts. Spoon into 8 well-greased 3½-inch custard cups; cover with foil; tie. Set in shallow pan on oven rack; add boiling water to come halfway up sides of cups. Bake 1½ hours. Cool on rack 5 minutes. Unmold. Serve with foamy or other favorite sauce. Makes 8 servings.

COCONUT STEAMED PUDDING

½ cup all-purpose flour,
sifted before measuring
1 teaspoon double-acting baking powder
¾ teaspoon salt
1 teaspoon baking soda
½ teaspoon nutmeg
⅛ teaspoon ground cloves
1 teaspoon cinnamon
¾ cup shredded coconut, chopped fine
1 cup packed brown sugar
1 cup packaged dried bread crumbs
1 cup grated carrots
1 cup grated raw potatoes
1 cup finely diced,
peeled, cored cooking apples
½ cup light or dark raisins
¼ cup currants
¼ cup diced preserved orange peel
½ cup salad oil or melted shortening
1 egg, slightly beaten
Hard Sauce (page 51)

About 3 hours before serving: Grease 2-quart mold. Into large bowl, sift flour, baking powder, salt, soda, nutmeg, cloves and cinnamon. Add coconut and remaining ingredients except Hard Sauce; mix well. Spoon into mold; prepare to steam as in steps 3 and 4 of Cranberry Steamed Pudding (page 51). Cover; simmer 2 hours or until done. Serve with Hard Sauce or favorite pudding sauce. Makes about 10 servings.

To do ahead: Make pudding several days ahead; remove from mold; cool; wrap in foil and refrigerate. To serve, bake in foil wrapping at 325° F. for about 1 hour or until hot.

LIME CREAM SHERBET
pictured between pages 48-49

1 envelope unflavored gelatin
2 cups milk
½ teaspoon salt
1⅓ cups granulated sugar
2 cups light cream
2 tablespoons grated lime peel
½ cup lime juice
¼ cup lemon juice
green food color
6 thin lime slices

is for Ice creams, sherbets, ices and mousses

Up to 1 month ahead or early in day: In small bowl, sprinkle gelatin over ½ cup of the milk; let soften 5 minutes, then place bowl over boiling water and stir until gelatin dissolves.

In large bowl, combine remaining 1½ cups milk with salt, sugar, cream, lime peel, and lime and lemon juices; stir in gelatin and enough food color to tint mixture a delicate green. (If mixture appears to be curdled, don't worry; it disappears in freezing.) Chill 1 hour.

Pour mixture into 15½" by 10½" jelly-roll pan;* place in freezer until frozen 1 inch in from edge. Spoon into chilled large bowl; with electric mixer at medium speed, beat until smooth, but not melted. Return mixture to jelly-roll pan; freeze until firm. Cover with foil and keep frozen until ready to serve.

To serve: With tablespoon, scrape out enough shallow spoonfuls of sherbet to fill 6 sherbet glasses; give each lime slice a half twist and use to garnish sherbet. Makes 6 servings.

* Sherbet can be made in crank-type freezer following manufacturer's directions. Sherbet will be soft. Remove dasher and cover freezer can, or spoon sherbet into plastic or cardboard containers. Freeze.

BANANA CUPS

2 cups mashed bananas (about 3 bananas)
1 cup orange juice
2 tablespoons granulated sugar
1 teaspoon lemon juice

About 4 to 6 hours before serving: In medium bowl, combine ¼ cup water with bananas and remaining ingredients; mix well. Spoon into six 4-ounce paper cups; freeze until firm.

To serve: Let stand at room temperature for 5 minutes; peel off paper cups. Makes 6 servings.

HOMEMADE ICE CREAM
for crank-type freezer*

1½ cups milk
¾ cup granulated sugar
2 tablespoons all-purpose flour
⅛ teaspoon salt
2 eggs or 3 egg yolks
1½ cups heavy or whipping cream
1½ teaspoons vanilla extract

Up to 1 month before serving or early in day: In double boiler, heat milk until tiny bubbles appear around edge; do not boil. In medium bowl, combine sugar, flour and salt; stir in enough hot milk to make a smooth paste; stir paste into remaining milk in double boiler. Cook over medium heat, stirring, until thickened. Cover; cook 10 minutes.

In small bowl, beat eggs slightly; stirring constantly, slowly pour in some of the hot milk mixture; return all to double boiler. Cook 1 minute, stirring constantly. Remove from heat; let cool.

Stir cream and vanilla into cooled mixture; pour into freezer container and churn according to manufacturer's directions, using 1 part rock salt to 8 parts cracked ice. Ice cream will thicken in about ½ hour; it will be soft, not frozen. Remove dasher; cover can; place in freezer bucket or home freezer 2 to 3 hours to harden. Makes 1 quart.

* *To freeze in refrigerator freezing compartment:* Pour ice-cream mixture into 15½″ by 10½″ jelly-roll pan; place in freezer until frozen 1 inch in from edge. Spoon into large chilled bowl; with electric mixer at high speed, beat until smooth, but not melted. Pour into 9″ by 5″ pan. Freeze until firm; cover with foil; freeze.

⊷ BLUEBERRY-SWIRLED ICE CREAM: In covered electric-blender container, at low speed, blend *1 pint fresh blueberries, ¼ cup granulated sugar, 1 teaspoon lemon juice and 1 teaspoon allspice.* Prepare recipe as above, but omit the vanilla; stir blueberry mixture into soft ice cream; cover and allow to harden as above. Makes 1½ quarts.

⊷ SPICED BANANA ICE CREAM: In covered electric-blender container, at low speed, blend *4 ripe bananas* (if bananas are too ripe, flavor will be strong, color darker) with *2 teaspoons ascorbic-acid mixture* dissolved in *2 tablespoons water;* add *¼ cup granulated sugar* and *1 teaspoon cinnamon;* blend until smooth. Prepare recipe as above, but omit vanilla and add pureed bananas to cooled mixture before churning. Makes 1½ quarts.

ALMOND-FLAVORED ICE CREAM

1 tablespoon cornstarch
1½ cups milk
1½ cups light cream
1 tablespoon honey
⅓ cup granulated sugar
dash salt
2 teaspoons almond extract
3 eggs
Orange Sauce (page 125)

Day before serving: In double-boiler top, stir together cornstarch and ¼ cup of the milk until well blended. Add remaining milk, cream, honey, sugar, salt and almond extract, stirring until well blended. In cup, with wire whisk or fork, beat eggs well; beat into milk mixture until well blended. Cook over hot, *not boiling*, water, stirring constantly until mixture thickens slightly and coats a spoon, about ½ hour. Cover surface with waxed paper and refrigerate until cool, about 2 hours. Remove waxed paper; pour mixture into 6 custard cups or 1-quart mold. Freeze overnight.

Early in day: Unmold into sherbet dishes or onto serving platter; return to freezer until serving time. A few minutes before serving, remove from freezer to soften; serve with Orange Sauce. Makes about 6 servings.

FROZEN STRAWBERRY CREAM

2 pints sour cream
3 tablespoons lemon juice
1⅓ cups granulated sugar
2 pints strawberries, washed and hulled
¾ cup finely chopped walnuts

Day before or early in day: In 13″ by 9″ pan, combine sour cream, lemon juice and sugar.

In covered electric-blender container, at medium speed, blend about 1 cup of the strawberries at a time until coarsely pureed. Or put berries through sieve or food mill. Stir into sour-cream mixture until well blended. Cover pan with plastic wrap or foil and freeze until almost firm, about 2 hours.

Spoon into chilled large bowl; with electric mixer at medium speed, beat until mixture is smooth. Spoon into twelve 5- or 6-ounce custard cups. Sprinkle nuts over ice cream. Cover and freeze until firm. Makes 12 servings.

FRESH-STRAWBERRY FROST

3 pints hulled fresh strawberries
2 cups granulated sugar
1½ cups orange juice
½ cup lemon juice
¼ cup Grand Marnier

Several days before serving: In electric-blender container, put half of strawberries and half of sugar, orange juice and lemon juice. Cover blender container; blend 30 seconds. Turn mixture into 12″ by 8″ baking dish.

Repeat, using remaining strawberries, sugar and juices. Or put through food mill or press through sieve.

Stir in Grand Marnier, then freeze until partially frozen. Turn into bowl; with electric mixer at medium speed, beat until smooth; return mixture to baking dish and freeze until firm. Cover with foil; store in freezer. Its tart flavor mellows with refreezing.

To serve: Remove from freezer about 10 minutes or until soft enough to spoon into sherbet glasses. Makes 8 to 10 servings.

FRUITED SHERBET BALLS

3 pints lemon, lime, raspberry
or orange sherbet
1 8¾-ounce can pitted dark cherries
¼ teaspoon ground cloves
¼ teaspoon cinnamon
1 11-ounce can mandarin-orange sections
1 16-ounce can cling-peach slices
1½ cups seedless green grapes
1 cup combined syrups
drained from peaches and mandarin oranges

Day before serving: With ice-cream scoop, make sherbet balls; place on chilled cookie sheet. Cover with plastic wrap; freeze.

In skillet, heat cherries, cloves, cinnamon; simmer 5 minutes: Stir in oranges, peaches, grapes, peach and orange syrups. Cover, then refrigerate.

Just before serving: Arrange sherbet balls in sherbet dishes; spoon some sauce over each and serve at once. Makes 12 servings.

MILLICENT'S LEMON CRÈME

1 lemon
1 cup granulated sugar
1 envelope unflavored gelatin
1½ cups milk
2 teaspoons vanilla extract
dash salt
1 cup heavy or whipping cream

About 4 to 6 hours before serving: Finely grate all peel from lemon. Slice lemon; remove seeds, then into bowl, with scissors, cut lemon slices finely.

In small saucepan, mix grated lemon peel, cut-up lemon with juice and ½ cup of the sugar; heat gently until sugar is dissolved.

In large bowl, soften gelatin in ¾ cup of the milk for 5 minutes. Meanwhile, scald remaining ¾ cup milk with remaining ½ cup sugar. Stir hot milk into gelatin mixture until gelatin is dissolved. Slowly stir in sugar-lemon mixture, then vanilla and salt. In same bowl, freeze until firm about 2 inches in around edge.

In medium bowl, whip cream, then beat frozen mixture until smooth. Carefully fold whipped cream into smooth lemon mixture. Freeze until firm. Makes 1 quart or 8 servings.

⊷§ LOW-CALORIE LEMON CRÈME: Prepare as above, but substitute skimmed milk for whole milk and evaporated skimmed milk for cream.

In medium bowl, freeze 1 cup evaporated skimmed milk until ice crystals form 1 inch in from edge of bowl. Whip until consistency of whipped cream and fold into smooth lemon mixture as above. Makes 1½ quarts or 12 servings.

APRICOT ICE

2 30-ounce cans peeled whole apricots
2¼ cups orange juice
⅓ cup lemon juice
1 cup granulated sugar

About 2 hours before churning ice cream: Drain apricots; remove pits; puree pulp in electric-blender container, food mill or sieve.

Stir together apricot puree, orange juice, lemon juice and sugar until sugar is dissolved. Refrigerate until chilled, about 1 hour.

Churn and freeze in ice-cream maker as manufacturer directs. Makes 1½ quarts or 12 servings.

PEACH CREAM

1 14½-ounce can evaporated skimmed milk
1 envelope unflavored gelatin
2 tablespoons lemon juice
2 cups sliced fresh peaches
1 cup granulated sugar
1 teaspoon vanilla extract

About 1 hour before churning ice cream: Into large bowl, empty evaporated milk. Place bowl and electric-mixer beaters in freezer until ice crystals have formed about 1 inch in from edge of bowl.

Meanwhile, in small saucepan, mix gelatin and lemon juice; let stand 5 minutes to soften. Heat gently over low heat until gelatin has just dissolved.

In electric-blender container, place gelatin mixture and peaches; cover; blend at high speed to form a smooth puree. Add sugar and vanilla; blend until sugar is dissolved. (Or peaches may be pureed with sieve or food mill and mixed with gelatin mixture, sugar and vanilla.)

With electric mixer at high speed, beat chilled milk until the consistency of whipped cream. Gently fold in peach mixture. Chill for 1 hour. Churn and freeze in ice-cream maker as manufacturer directs. Makes 1½ quarts or 12 servings.

ᴇᴈ STRAWBERRY CREAM: Substitute 1 pint fresh strawberries for peaches; prepare as directed for Peach Cream, above.

CHOCOLATE-CONE SUNDAE

Several days before serving: Using large ice-cream scoop, make 6 coffee ice-cream balls; place in shallow dish; freezer-wrap and freeze.

About 1½ hours before serving: In double-boiler top, over hot, *not boiling*, water, melt *one 6-ounce package semisweet-chocolate pieces* with *1 tablespoon butter or margarine*. Stir in *5 large marshmallows*, finely chopped with scissors, until almost melted; then stir in, until well coated, *1½ cups cornflakes*, coarsely crushed and *½ cup flaked coconut*.

With teaspoon, lightly press this mixture to bottom and sides of six well-buttered, 6-ounce custard cups; refrigerate 1 hour.

About ½ hour before serving: With small spatula, carefully loosen baskets from custard cups; let stand at room temperature 25 minutes; let ice-cream balls stand at room temperature for about 15 minutes. Place each chocolate basket in sauce dish or on dessert plate. Now top each basket with coffee ice-cream ball; drizzle on *caramel topping* (from jar) and serve at once. Makes 6 servings.

BIG-TOP SUNDAE
pictured between pages 48-49

Early in day: Run sharp knife down around inside edge of *6 round pint containers of vanilla ice cream;* gently ease ice cream out of containers in one piece; place on tray; cover with foil; freeze.

At serving time: In punch bowl, place 2 pints of the ice cream; over it, sprinkle some of *one 3½-ounce package buttered, salted popcorn.* Top with remaining ice cream and popcorn; drizzle with your favorite *chocolate* or *caramel sauce;* pass additional sauce. Makes 18 servings.

RAINBOW ROLLS

Several days ahead or early in day: Line 15½″ by 10½″ jelly-roll pan with waxed paper; extend waxed paper about 2 inches beyond each short side of pan. Refrigerate until well chilled. Spread *2 pints raspberry sherbet,* softened, evenly in bottom of chilled pan; freeze until firm, about 3 hours. Then spread *2 pints orange sherbet,* softened, evenly over raspberry; freeze until firm, but not solid, about 3 hours. (When frozen solid, sherbet does not roll well.)

To roll, with spatula, loosen long sides of sherbet from waxed paper. Working quickly, in jelly-roll fashion, lift narrow end of waxed paper and turn over end of sherbet, pressing with fingers to start roll. Peel paper back, then continue lifting paper and rolling sherbet until completely rolled. Discard paper. (If necessary, use spatula to help separate paper from sherbet as you roll.)

Quickly place roll, seam side down, on freezer-proof platter. Return to freezer until serving time. Makes 8 servings.

◆§ OTHER COMBINATIONS: *Chocolate* and *pistachio ice cream; lime* and *lemon sherbets;* or *strawberry* and *vanilla ice cream.*

VANILLA-AND-COFFEE ICE CREAM GOURMET

2 pints each vanilla
and coffee ice cream
½ cup chocolate sauce
½ cup sour cream

Early in day: With ice-cream scoop or large spoon, scoop out 4 balls of ice cream from each pint. Arrange in jelly-roll pan; freeze. Mix sauce and sour cream; cover; refrigerate.

Just before serving: Arrange balls of ice cream in pretty bowl. Spoon chocolate-sour-cream sauce over all. Makes 8 servings.

FROZEN APPLE CREAM

¼ lemon, cut into 3 pieces
2 cups canned applesauce
1 8-ounce package cream cheese
¾ cup granulated sugar
1 teaspoon vanilla extract
1 cup heavy or whipping cream

Up to 2 weeks before serving: Place lemon in covered electric-blender container; blend 30 seconds. Add half of the applesauce, cheese, sugar and vanilla; blend 60 seconds. Add remaining applesauce; blend smooth. Stir in cream; pour into 10″ by 6″ pan; place in freezer until frozen 1 inch in from edge. Spoon mixture back into blender container; blend smooth. Pour back into pan; freezer-wrap and freeze until firm.

About 15 minutes before serving: Remove from freezer; let stand at room temperature until soft enough to spoon into serving dishes. Makes 8 servings.

SHERBET-CREAM BOMBE

1 pint pistachio ice cream
1 pint chocolate-chip ice cream
1 pint orange sherbet
1½ pints raspberry sherbet
1½ cups heavy or whipping cream

About 1 week before serving: Slightly soften pistachio ice cream and spoon into bottom of 2-quart melon mold or freezerproof bowl. Place in freezer, being sure it stands level, for 1 hour. Meanwhile, soften chocolate-chip ice cream; spread in even layer over pistachio; freeze. Repeat with layers of orange and raspberry sherbets. When frozen, cover and store in freezer.

About 2 hours before serving: Quickly dip mold in warm water; invert freezerproof serving plate on mold; invert both. Lift off mold; refreeze bombe. In medium bowl, with electric mixer at high speed, whip cream until stiff peaks form; "frost" bombe with whipped cream. Keep in freezer until ready to serve. Makes 12 servings.

⇜ SHERBET-CREAM CAKE: Instead of layering ice cream, scoop balls from pistachio ice cream, orange and raspberry sherbets. Beat chocolate-chip ice cream until like a heavy batter. Arrange layers of ice cream and sherbet balls in 9-inch angel-food-cake pan and pour ice cream "batter" around balls. Freeze, then frost with whipped cream.

RICH FRUIT CREAM TARTS

½ cup granulated sugar
¼ teaspoon salt
¼ cup all-purpose flour
2 cups milk
1 teaspoon vanilla extract
2 eggs
2 cups crumbled macaroons
1 cup chopped pecans
½ cup chopped candied cherries
½ cup heavy or whipping cream

Two weeks before serving: In medium saucepan, combine sugar, salt, flour; stir in milk and vanilla. Cook over high heat, stirring constantly until mixture boils and thickens. In cup, beat eggs, then beat some of hot mixture into eggs; pour into mixture in saucepan and continue stirring and cooking a few minutes longer. Stir in macaroons, pecans and cherries; refrigerate.

In bowl, whip cream until stiff; fold into chilled macaroon mixture; spoon into 12 to 16 paper baking cups; cover with plastic wrap or foil; freeze. Makes 12 to 16 servings.

PINK PEPPERMINT ICE CREAM
for crank-type freezer

½ pound peppermint-stick candy
2 cups milk
1 cup heavy or whipping cream
1 cup light cream

About 3 hours before churning ice cream: Place candy between sheets of waxed paper or in heavy plastic bag; with rolling pin, pound candy to a fine powder. In bowl, combine candy and milk; refrigerate for 2 hours, stirring occasionally.

To candy mixture, add heavy and light cream. Chill for 1 hour. Pour into freezer container and churn according to manufacturer's directions. Makes 1½ quarts or 12 servings.

LOW-CALORIE PEPPERMINT ICE CREAM: Prepare as above, but use only 6 ounces of peppermint candy, and substitute 2 cups skimmed milk for whole milk and 2 cups evaporated skimmed milk for creams. For a milder flavor, reduce candy to 4 ounces and add ⅓ cup granulated sugar.

RASPBERRY SNOWBALL
pictured between pages 48-49

¾ cup granulated sugar
1 envelope unflavored gelatin
6 egg yolks
¼ cup light rum (optional)
4 cups heavy or whipping cream
3 pints raspberry sherbet,
slightly softened

Up to 1 week before or day before serving: Place 2½-quart mixing bowl in freezer to chill.

Meanwhile, in saucepan, combine sugar with ¾ cup water; stir until dissolved. Bring to boiling; boil 5 minutes. Remove from heat; cool without stirring.

In measuring cup, over ¼ cup water, sprinkle gelatin to soften. Place cup in hot water and stir until gelatin is dissolved.

In double-boiler top, with electric mixer at high speed, beat egg yolks until light and lemon colored; gradually beat in cooled syrup. Cook over hot, *not boiling*, water, until creamy and thick. Remove from heat; stir in gelatin mixture, then rum, if desired. Place saucepan in bowl of ice cubes and stir mixture constantly until cool. Whip 2 cups of the cream; gently fold into cooled gelatin mixture. Pour into large shallow pan; place in freezer until just set.

Meanwhile, completely line chilled mixing bowl with ¾-inch- to 1-inch-thick shell of raspberry sherbet, spreading it evenly over bottom and up sides. (If sherbet becomes too soft to work with while bowl is being lined, return bowl and sherbet to freezer until firm.) When bowl is lined, freeze until firm.

Fill frozen raspberry shell with the set whipped cream mixture, packing it in firmly and smoothing off top. Cover with foil and freeze for at least 12 hours.

Early in day: To unmold snowball: Quickly dip bowl into very hot water just to rim for about 10 seconds; lift bowl from water; dry. Invert chilled serving plate on top of bowl; quickly invert bowl and plate and lift off bowl. Place in freezer.

Whip remaining 2 cups of cream until very stiff; spread evenly over frozen snowball, reserving some of the cream for garnish; return snowball to freezer. Meanwhile, fill pastry bag with rest of whipped cream. Using tube no. 28, pipe cream in small rosettes, close together, all over snowball. If snowball or whipped cream becomes slightly soft, return to freezer until firm, then continue until snowball is covered. Freeze until firm.

To serve: With silver knife dipped in hot water, cut into wedges. Makes 12 servings.

FRENCH HEART-OF-CREAM WITH PEACH SAUCE

1½ cups heavy or whipping cream
6 egg yolks
½ cup granulated sugar
1 teaspoon vanilla extract
Peach Sauce (below)

Early in day or day before: In small bowl, with electric mixer at high speed, whip cream until soft peaks form. Wash beaters.

In large bowl, with electric mixer at high speed, beat yolks and sugar until thick and lemon colored. Beat in vanilla. Fold in whipped cream. Pour into 6-cup heart-shaped mold; freeze until firm.

To serve: Unmold; serve with Peach Sauce. Makes 10 to 12 servings.

Peach Sauce: In covered electric-blender container at low speed, blend *two 10-ounce packages frozen peaches, thawed, ½ teaspoon almond extract, ¼ teaspoon nutmeg.*

FROZEN BLUEBERRY MOUSSE

2 10-ounce packages
frozen blueberries, thawed
¾ cup granulated sugar
1 tablespoon lemon juice
2 envelopes unflavored gelatin
3 cups heavy or whipping cream
blueberries for garnish

Up to 1 month before serving: Put 2- or 2½-quart decorative mold in refrigerator to chill. In covered electric-blender container, finely puree blueberries, one package at a time, pouring puree into large bowl. Add sugar and lemon juice and stir until sugar is completely dissolved.

Soften gelatin in ½ cup cold water; dissolve over hot water; stir into blueberry puree. Stir until mixture begins to thicken.

Whip 2 cups of the cream until it peaks; fold into blueberry puree. Pour mixture into chilled mold; refrigerate for 1 hour, then cover with foil and place in freezer.

In bowl, whip remaining 1 cup cream until stiff; place in decorating bag; with decorating tube number 7, make 10 rosettes on foil-covered cookie sheet. Freeze rosettes, uncovered; when frozen, lay carefully, in freezer-type carton, or wrap in foil.

About 5 hours before serving: Remove mousse from freezer; unmold onto serving dish; refrigerate. One hour before serving, decorate mousse with frozen cream rosettes; refrigerate. At serving time, if desired, garnish mousse with blueberries. Makes about 10 servings.

BAKED ALASKA
pictured between pages 80-81

2 pints lemon sherbet
1 15.5-ounce package brownie mix
2 pints orange sherbet
8 egg whites
1 cup granulated sugar
2 tablespoons chocolate sauce

From 1 to 7 days before serving: Line 1½-quart mixing bowl with waxed paper, leaving a 2-inch overhang at top. Press the lemon sherbet into mixing bowl with bottom of a 3-cup bowl, so it completely lines mixing bowl. Leave 3-cup bowl in place; freeze until sherbet is firm.

Meanwhile, make up brownie mix as label directs for cake-type brownies; pour into 9-inch layer-cake pan. Bake the longer time label directs; cool on rack, then freezer-wrap and freeze.

When sherbet is firm, remove 3-cup bowl by filling it with hot water to loosen. Fill cavity left by bowl with orange sherbet; freeze.

Several hours before serving: Cut circle of brown paper 1-inch larger in diameter than brownie layer; place on ungreased cookie sheet. Un-wrap frozen brownie; center on paper circle. With spatula, loosen sherbet in bowl; unmold onto brownie; remove waxed paper; return to freezer.

About ½ hour before serving: In large bowl, with electric mixer at high speed, beat egg whites until foamy. Add 2 tablespoons of the sugar; beat at low speed 5 minutes. Repeat until all of the cup of sugar is added; continue beating at high speed until meringue holds stiff peaks when beater is raised. Meanwhile, preheat oven to 500° F.

Completely cover sherbet and brownie layer with meringue. Drizzle top of meringue with chocolate sauce, cutting through it several times with knife to give a marbled effect. Bake about 2 minutes, or just until lightly browned. Let stand about 5 minutes before cutting into wedges with a sharp knife dipped in hot water. Makes 16 wedges.

&§ YELLOW CAKE: Substitute 9-inch yellow-cake layer for brownie layer above. Use peppermint ice cream for outer layer, cherry vanilla or raspberry-swirl ice cream for inner layer. Stud meringue with slivered, blanched almonds.

&§ SPONGE CAKE: Substitute 9-inch spongecake layer for brownie layer above. Use strawberry ice cream for outer layer, pistachio ice cream for inner layer. Draw flat side of spatula through meringue at an angle to get swirled effect.

§ DEVIL'S FOOD CAKE: Substitute 9-inch devil's food-cake layer for brownie layer above. Use coffee ice cream for outer layer, fudge ripple or chocolate-chip ice cream for inner layer; sprinkle meringue with flaked coconut.

BROWNIE BAKED ALASKA

1 15.5-ounce package fudge-brownie mix
½ gallon brick vanilla ice cream,
sliced 1 inch thick
5 egg whites
dash salt
½ cup plus 2 tablespoons
granulated sugar
½ teaspoon vanilla extract

Several days before serving: Make and bake brownie mix as label directs; do not cut into squares. Cool, then invert on a freezer-and-oven proof platter.

Cover brownie square with ice cream slices, laid side by side. Freezer-wrap and freeze.

Shortly before serving: Preheat oven to 500° F. Beat egg whites with salt until moist peaks form; slowly add sugar, 2 tablespoons at a time, then vanilla, beating until stiff and glossy. Spread meringue over un-wrapped frozen brownie-ice-cream cake, swirling it into peaks on top. Bake 4 or 5 minutes; serve immediately. Makes 9 servings.

ICE CREAM POSIES

Up to 1 month before serving: Fill a chilled enamel, pottery or china pot de crème or demitasse cup with *your favorite ice cream or sherbet*; with edge of spatula, level off top. Place in freezer for ½ hour.

With number 20 ice-cream scoop, scoop up a ball of the same ice cream or sherbet; press it on top of filled cup from freezer; remove any drips from cup rim. With tip of teaspoon, make row of petal-like inden-tations about ⅛ inch apart all around base of ice-cream ball at cup rim. Make a second row of indentations just above the first, alternating these "petals." Continue making rows of petals until you reach top of ice-cream ball and have made a rose. If ice cream sticks to tip of spoon, dip it in cold water, wipe dry, and continue. Place "Posy" in freezer. When firm, cover with plastic wrap; freeze. Repeat for as many Posies as de-sired, using the same or different cream or sherbet.

About 15 to 25 minutes before serving: Unwrap Posies; set each on a chilled demitasse saucer. Let stand at room temperature to soften.

JELLY ROLL

¾ cup cake flour, sifted before measuring
¾ teaspoon double-acting baking powder
¼ teaspoon salt
4 eggs, at room temperature
granulated sugar
1 teaspoon vanilla extract
¾ cup strawberry jam
½ cup heavy or whipping cream

is for Jelly roll, in many disguises

About 1 hour before serving: Preheat oven to 400° F. With waxed paper, line bottom of 15½″ by 10½″ jelly-roll pan; lightly dust with flour. Sift together flour, baking powder and salt. In large bowl, with electric mixer at high speed, beat eggs until foamy; gradually beat in ¾ cup sugar; continue beating until very thick and lemon colored. With rubber spatula or wire whisk, fold in flour and vanilla. Turn into pan, spreading batter evenly. Bake 13 minutes or until light brown. Lift carefully from pan and cool, right side up, on rack for 5 minutes.

Meanwhile, dust 18-inch-long piece of waxed paper with ¼ cup granulated sugar. Turn top side of cake onto sugared paper; carefully peel paper from bottom and sides of cake. Trim edges; roll up with sugared paper from narrow end. Cool cake on rack, seam side down, ½ hour.

Just before serving: Whip cream; unroll jelly roll; remove waxed paper. Spread cake evenly with jam, then with whipped cream. Reroll and place on serving plate. Serve cut in 1-inch slices. Makes 8 to 10 servings.

PEACH CAKE ROLL
pictured between pages 80-81

2 tablespoons butter or margarine
1 19-ounce can peach-pie filling
1 tablespoon lemon juice
¼ teaspoon nutmeg
4 eggs, separated
granulated sugar
½ teaspoon vanilla extract
¾ cup all-purpose flour,
sifted before measuring
1 teaspoon double-acting baking powder
½ teaspoon salt
confectioners' sugar
hulled fresh strawberries

Several hours before serving: Preheat oven to 375° F. In oven, in 15½″ by 10½″ jelly-roll pan, melt butter to cover bottom of pan. Meanwhile, in small bowl, combine pie filling, lemon juice, nutmeg; spread evenly in pan; set aside.

In large bowl, with electric mixer at medium speed, beat egg yolks until thick and lemon colored; gradually beat in ½ cup granulated sugar and vanilla. In small bowl, with mixer at high speed, beat egg whites until soft peaks form; add ⅓ cup granulated sugar, about 2 table-spoons at a time, beating 5 minutes between additions; continue beating until stiff peaks form.

With rubber scraper, gently fold whites into yolks until no whites show. Sift together flour, baking powder and salt; fold into egg mixture until thoroughly blended. Gently spread batter evenly over pie filling; bake 20 minutes or until cake springs back when pressed gently with finger.

Meanwhile, sprinkle a clean tea towel with about ⅓ cup confectioners' sugar. When cake is done, immediately loosen edges with small metal spatula and quickly invert onto tea towel. If any filling remains in pan, remove it and spread on cake. Let stand 3 minutes. Then, using towel to help, roll up cake; let stand 10 minutes. With wide spatulas, carefully transfer to cake plate; cool.

Before serving, sift confectioners' sugar over roll and arrange straw-berries around it. To serve, cut into 1-inch slices, serving each with a berry or two. Makes 10 servings.

ALMOND-STUDDED JELLY ROLL

Early in day: Preheat oven to 350° F. Line bottom of 15½″ by 10½″ jelly-roll pan and 8-inch layer-cake pan with waxed paper; don't grease.

Prepare *one 16-ounce package angel-food-cake mix* as label directs; place 3 cups of the batter in 8-inch pan and spread remaining batter in jelly-roll pan. Bake both cakes 20 minutes or until they spring back when gently pressed with finger. Cool in pans, on racks, 10 minutes. Carefully loosen edges with spatula; invert each cake on clean tea towel; lift off pans. Peel off paper from both cakes. Wrap and freeze 8-inch cake for later use.

Gently roll up jelly-roll with towel. Cool thoroughly, seam side down, on rack for about 1½ hours. Unroll cake and spread surface evenly to within about 1 inch of edges with *one 12-ounce jar apricot preserves.* Carefully reroll cake; place, seam side down, on serving plate.

In bowl, blend *one 8-ounce package of cream cheese,* softened, with *½ pint sour cream;* spread over jelly roll. Stick *toasted, slivered almond slices* into frosting in random pattern until roll is completely covered. Refrigerate. Makes 10 servings.

PINK CLOUD CAKE

1¾ cups all-purpose flour,
sifted before measuring
¼ teaspoon salt
½ teaspoon double-acting baking powder
7 eggs
1½ cups granulated sugar
1 tablespoon grated lemon peel
⅓ cup salad oil
confectioners' sugar
1½ cups raspberry preserves
2 2-ounce packages whipped-topping mix

Early in day: Line two greased 8-inch layer-cake pans and one greased 15½″ by 10½″ jelly-roll pan with waxed paper; grease papers, then lightly dust with flour; set aside.

Sift flour, salt and baking powder together. Preheat oven to 375° F.

In large bowl, with electric mixer at medium speed, beat eggs until light and fluffy; continuing to beat, gradually add granulated sugar and lemon peel, beating until thick and lemon colored. Alternately fold in, about one-fourth of each at a time, flour mixture and oil, just until smooth. Pour 2 cups of batter into each 8-inch pan; spread remaining batter in jelly-roll pan. Bake all 3 cakes 18 to 20 minutes or until cakes spring back when lightly pressed with finger.

While layers bake, sprinkle 18-inch-long piece of waxed paper with confectioners' sugar. As soon as jelly-roll layer comes out of oven, loosen from sides of pan; invert on sugared paper. Peel off waxed paper from sides and bottom; trim cake edges.

Cool the two 8-inch layers in pans on racks 10 minutes; invert on racks; remove waxed paper; cool completely.

Meanwhile, spread jelly-roll layer with ½ cup of the preserves; cut into six 15″ by 1½″ strips. Roll up one of the strips, jelly-roll fashion, and place, cut side down, in center of large round plate. Then wind the other 5 strips around the center roll, forming an 8-inch pinwheel layer.

Prepare whipped topping, one package at a time, as label directs; fold ½ cup of preserves into each batch.

On cake plate, arrange 4 strips of waxed paper around edges to form a square; place one 8-inch layer in center; spread with ½ cup topping mixture. With 2 broad spatulas, lift pinwheel layer and place on top of first layer; spread with ½ cup topping mixture; top with second 8-inch layer. Frost top and sides of cake with remaining topping mixture. Remove paper strips. Refrigerate. Makes 12 servings.

BAVARIAN JELLY ROLL

1 4-ounce package chocolate-fudge
pudding-and-pie filling
1½ cups milk
2 egg yolks, slightly beaten
2 teaspoons orange extract
¾ cup cake flour, sifted before measuring
1 teaspoon double-acting baking powder
¼ teaspoon salt
4 eggs, at room temperature
granulated sugar
4 teaspoons almond extract
2 3½-ounce packages vanilla-flavor
whipped-dessert mix
2 cups heavy or whipping cream

Day before serving: In saucepan, combine pudding with 1½ cups milk; stir in egg yolks and orange extract. Cook over medium heat, stirring, until mixture comes to boiling. Pour into large bowl; place waxed paper directly on surface of pudding; refrigerate.

Preheat oven to 400° F. Prepare two jelly rolls, one at a time. For each, line one greased 15½" by 10½" jelly-roll pan with waxed paper; grease paper. Sift ¼ cup plus 2 tablespoons of the cake flour with ½ teaspoon of the baking powder and ⅛ teaspoon of the salt.

In small bowl, with electric mixer at high speed, beat 2 of the eggs until foamy; add ⅓ cup sugar, continuing to beat until thick and lemon colored; with spatula or whisk, quickly fold in flour and 1 teaspoon of the almond extract. Spread evenly in jelly-roll pan. Bake 8 minutes or until light brown.

Lightly dust a clean tea towel with granulated sugar. When cake is done, loosen it from sides of pan; invert onto towel; carefully peel off waxed paper; with knife, trim cake edges. Gently roll cake and towel together, jelly-roll fashion, from long side. Cool 10 minutes.

Bake second jelly roll as above, using the remaining flour, baking powder, salt and eggs with ⅓ cup sugar and 1 teaspoon of the almond extract.

Unroll jelly rolls so each is on its own towel. Gently lift and move one jelly roll next to the other so that longer sides overlap about 1 inch. Spread evenly with chocolate filling. Starting from shorter side, roll up tightly as one cake, jelly-roll fashion. Cover and refrigerate.

Early in day: With sharp knife, slice jelly roll into 9 even crosswise slices. In bottom of oiled 9-cup soufflé dish, center 1 slice, cut side down, with 4 more slices laid around it, in spoke-like fashion, equidistantly apart.

Prepare 1 package of the dessert mix as label directs; fold in 1 cup of the cream, whipped with 1 teaspoon of the almond extract; spoon into cake-lined soufflé dish. Place 4 jelly-roll slices on end, against and around inside of soufflé dish, equidistantly apart. Prepare remaining dessert whip with whipped cream and almond extract as above. Pour into soufflé dish; refrigerate 4 hours or until serving time.

Just before serving: Set soufflé dish, just up to the rim, in warm water. Lift from water and shake slightly to loosen cream and cake from dish. Unmold onto large round serving platter. Makes 10 servings.

MINI NESSEL-ROLLS

1 18.5-ounce package
orange chiffon-cake mix
confectioners' sugar
1 cup frozen whipped topping
2 tablespoons chopped, mixed candied fruit
1 tablespoon grated orange peel
¼ teaspoon rum extract

Early in day: Preheat oven to 350° F. Line 15½" by 10½" jelly-roll pan with waxed paper; grease and flour. Line 9" by 5" loaf pan with waxed paper. Prepare cake mix as label directs, but pour half of batter into jelly-roll pan and remaining batter into loaf pan. Bake jelly roll 12 to 15 minutes or until cake comes away from sides of pan. Bake loaf 40 minutes more; cool in pan; wrap and freeze to serve later.

While jelly roll bakes, sift thin layer of confectioners' sugar onto 18-inch length of waxed paper. Cut another 18-inch length of waxed paper in half lengthwise, then crosswise to make quarters; set aside. As soon as jelly roll is done, loosen edges from sides of pan; invert onto sugared paper. Quickly peel off paper; sift thin layer of confectioners' sugar over cake.

With sharp knife, cut cake in half lengthwise, then crosswise to make quarters. (With scissors, cut waxed paper beneath cake, too.) Place reserved waxed papers over cake pieces. Starting with long edge, tightly roll each cake piece up, jelly-roll fashion, with waxed paper; place rolls close together, seam side down, on rack to cool.

While cake cools, in small bowl, combine thawed frozen topping with candied fruit, orange peel and rum extract.

Unroll cake and remove waxed paper. Spread ¼ cup filling in center of cake, almost to edges. Reroll cake just so edges touch, holding edges together for a few seconds to help seal. Place, seam side down, on cutting board and cut into thirds. Repeat with remaining rolls; cover with plastic wrap; refrigerate.

Just before serving: Sift thin layer of confectioners' sugar over the top of the rolls. Makes 12 servings.

FRUITED SAVARIN

½ lemon
½ cup lemon-lime carbonated beverage
⅓ cup honey
salt
½ cup sherry
1 small apple and pear
1 orange, peeled
⅔ cup milk
2 tablespoons butter or margarine
1 tablespoon granulated sugar
1½ teaspoons active dry yeast
2 eggs, beaten
2 cups all-purpose flour,
sifted before measuring

K is for Kuchen and other yeast-dough delights

Early in day: Grate 1 tablespoon of lemon peel; set aside. Into small bowl, squeeze 1 tablespoon of lemon juice; combine with beverage, honey, ½ teaspoon salt and sherry. Core and thinly slice unpeeled apple and pear; cut sections from orange; place all fruit in honey mixture; refrigerate. Grease 6-cup ring mold; set aside.

In saucepan, warm milk; add butter; stir until melted. Add ¼ teaspoon salt, sugar, grated peel, yeast, eggs and flour; beat until batter is smooth. Spread in ring mold; cover with damp cloth and let rise in warm place (80° to 85° F.) until doubled, about 45 minutes.

Preheat oven to 425° F. Bake ring mold 15 minutes or until golden. Cool on rack 10 minutes; loosen with spatula; turn onto serving plate. Drain fruit; slowly drizzle honey mixture over ring; let set until serving time, spooning honey mixture over it several times.

At serving time: Spoon fruit into center of ring. Makes 8 servings.

CHERRY KUCHEN

about 3 cups all-purpose flour
¼ cup granulated sugar
1 teaspoon salt
1 package active dry yeast
½ cup sour cream
2 tablespoons butter or margarine
1 egg
2 21- or 22-ounce cans cherry-pie filling

Early in day: In large bowl, combine 1 cup of the flour, sugar, salt and dry yeast. In saucepan, heat ½ cup water with cream and butter until very warm (120° to 130° F.). Butter need not melt. With electric mixer at medium speed, gradually add to flour mixture; beat 2 minutes, scraping bowl occasionally; add ½ cup of the flour and egg; beat at high speed 2 minutes. Stir in about 1¼ cups flour to make soft dough. Knead on lightly floured surface 10 minutes, or until smooth and elastic. Place in large greased bowl; turn to grease top. Cover; let rise in warm place (80° to 85° F.) until doubled, about 1½ hours.

Preheat oven to 375° F. Punch down dough; reserve ⅓ for top. Pat remaining dough into bottom and sides of greased 13″ by 9″ baking pan. Spread evenly with pie filling. Roll out reserved dough; cut into 10 strips; cover cherries in lattice fashion; pinch edges all around to seal. Bake 35 minutes. Serve cut into squares. Makes 12 servings.

CHEESE COFFEE-CAKE RING

2 13¾-ounce packages hot-roll mix
granulated sugar
5 egg yolks
1 cup sour cream
½ cup melted butter or margarine
1 8-ounce package cream cheese
2 eggs
1 teaspoon vanilla extract
1 10-ounce jar apricot jam
¼ cup chopped pistachio nuts

Early in day: In ½ cup warm water, dissolve yeast from both packages of hot-roll mix. In large bowl, combine flour from both packages with ½ cup sugar. In bowl, beat egg yolks until light; stir in sour cream, butter and dissolved yeast; gradually stir into flour mixture, beating until dough is soft and smooth. Place in large greased bowl, turning over to grease top. Cover with towel; let rise in warm place (80° to 85° F.) until doubled, about 1½ hours.

Meanwhile, in bowl, with electric mixer at medium speed, beat cheese until fluffy; add ½ cup sugar, eggs, one at a time, and vanilla.

Punch down dough; knead lightly. On lightly floured surface, roll dough into 18-inch circle; carefully lay it over a greased 3-quart ring mold; ease dough down to line bottom and sides, being careful not to make holes. Pour in cheese filling. Lap outer edges of dough over filling, pressing to dough on inner ring to seal. Cut cross in dough which covers hole in center; fold cross-formed triangles back over ring. Let dough rise to top of mold. Preheat oven to 350° F. Bake 40 minutes or until golden. Invert mold on rack; cool 10 minutes, then lift off mold.

In small saucepan, melt apricot jam; using pastry brush, coat cake with jam. Sprinkle with nuts. Cool completely. Makes 18 servings.

BABA AU RHUM
pictured between pages 80-81

all-purpose flour
¼ cup granulated sugar
1 package active dry yeast
½ cup milk
¼ cup butter or margarine
3 eggs
2 tablespoons candied citron
2 tablespoons dark raisins
2 tablespoons orange juice
3 tablespoons lemon juice
1 cup light corn syrup
1 cup white rum
½ cup apricot preserves
candied cherries

1. *Early in day:* In large mixing bowl, combine ⅔ cup flour, sugar and yeast. In medium saucepan, heat milk and butter until very warm (120° to 130° F.). Butter does not need to melt. With electric mixer at medium speed, gradually add liquid to flour mixture. Beat 2 minutes, scraping bowl occasionally. Add ½ cup flour and eggs; beat 2 minutes at high speed, scraping bowl occasionally.
2. With spoon, stir in enough additional flour to make a thick batter.
3. Add citron and raisins. Cover bowl with towel; let rise in warm place (80° to 85° F.) away from draft until doubled, about 1 hour.
4. Punch down dough by pushing down center with fist, then pushing edges into center. Divide dough evenly among 16 well-greased ⅔-cup china custard cups or 3-inch muffin-pan cups. Cover with towel; let rise in warm place until doubled, about 1 hour.
5. Preheat oven to 375° F. Place custard cups on 2 cookie sheets. Stagger pans in oven so that they are not directly above each other. Bake 20 to 25 minutes or until golden brown. Cover tops with foil if they tend to become too dark. Let stand 5 minutes before removing to racks. When cool, place in roasting pan, bottom side up.
6. To make sauce, combine orange juice and 2 tablespoons of the lemon juice, corn syrup, rum; spoon over babas until all sauce is absorbed. Let stand for at least 2 hours at room temperature.

Just before serving: Combine apricot preserves with 1 tablespoon lemon juice; brush top and sides of babas; top with a candied cherry. Place on individual serving dishes. Makes 16 servings.

⊷§ EASY BABA AU RHUM: For dough in steps 1 to 2, substitute two 13¾-ounce packages hot-roll mix prepared as label directs, adding 2 egg yolks and ¼ cup granulated sugar. Add citron and raisins as in step 3; let rise and continue as above.

GIANT BLUEBERRY TART

1 13¾-ounce package hot-roll mix
¾ cup warm milk
¼ cup butter or margarine, melted
1½ cups granulated sugar
3 eggs
2 cups all-purpose flour,
sifted before measuring
11 cups fresh blueberries, or six 10-ounce packages
frozen, unsweetened blueberries, thawed and drained
3 tablespoons cornstarch
grated peel of 1 lemon

Early in day: In large bowl, dissolve yeast from roll mix in ¼ cup warm water. Stir in milk; butter; ½ cup of the sugar; 2 of the eggs, beaten; flour; and flour from roll mix. Knead dough in bowl until smooth; cover; let rise in warm place (80° to 85° F.) until doubled.

Punch down dough; on floured surface, knead until smooth and elastic; cut off ¼ of dough and set aside. Roll remaining dough into 18" by 16" rectangle; line bottom and sides of 15½" by 10½" jelly-roll pan. In large bowl, combine blueberries, cornstarch, remaining 1 cup sugar and lemon peel; spoon into jelly-roll pan. Preheat oven to 350° F.

Roll reserved dough into 17" by 15" rectangle; cut into fourteen 16" by 1" strips. Lay 1 strip diagonally across pan from corner to corner. On each side of it, lay 2 parallel strips, 2½ inches apart. Repeat strips in opposite direction, for diamond effect. Trim overhanging dough even with pan edges; brush with beaten egg. Lay remaining pastry strips around top edges; brush with egg; let rise 15 minutes.

Bake 25 minutes; cover with foil and bake 20 minutes more. Nice served warm or cold with whipped cream. Makes 12 generous servings.

HOLIDAY KRINGEL

½ cup butter or margarine
½ cup milk
2 to 2½ cups all-purpose flour
½ teaspoon salt
1½ tablespoons granulated sugar
1 package active dry yeast
1 egg, separated
1 cup each finely chopped
candied cherries and almonds
confectioners' sugar

Early in day: In saucepan, heat ¼ cup water with butter and milk until very warm (120° to 130° F.). Butter does not need to melt. In large bowl, combine ½ cup of the flour with salt, sugar and yeast. With electric mixer at medium speed, gradually add milk mixture; beat 2 minutes, scraping bowl occasionally. Add egg yolk; beat 2 minutes. With spoon, stir in enough flour to make a soft dough. Knead on lightly floured surface until smooth and elastic, about 10 minutes. Shape into ball; place in large greased bowl, turning dough to grease top. Cover; refrigerate 2 to 48 hours.

About 2 hours before baking: In bowl, combine cherries and almonds. On lightly floured surface, roll half of dough into 18″ by 6″ rectangle. Brush with half of egg white and spread with half of cherry-nut mixture. Fold long sides to center over filling; pinch edges together; cut in half crosswise; place the two 9-inch lengths, seam side down, on lightly greased cookie sheet. Repeat with remaining dough, placing the two 9-inch lengths on another cookie sheet. Cover; let rise in warm place (80° to 85° F.) until doubled, for ½ to 1½ hours.

Preheat oven to 400° F. Bake 20 minutes, or until golden. Sprinkle with confectioners' sugar. Cut into 1-inch slices. Makes 32 slices.

GLAZED GRAPE KUCHEN

1 8-ounce package refrigerated
crescent rolls
1 teaspoon cinnamon
1 tablespoon granulated sugar
¼ teaspoon nutmeg
½ cup vanilla-wafer crumbs
2 cups seedless grapes
3 tablespoons melted butter or margarine
⅓ cup apricot jam

About 1 hour before serving: Preheat oven to 400° F. Unroll crescent rolls. Lay the 2 strips of dough lengthwise, side by side, in greased 12″ by 8″ baking dish, rolling up ends to fit dish. Combine cinnamon, sugar, nutmeg and crumbs; sprinkle over dough; top with grapes, then drizzle with butter. Bake ½ hour or until bottom is golden.

Combine apricot jam with 1 tablespoon water to make glaze; brush over grapes. Serve warm, cut into squares, as is or topped with a bit of ice cream. Makes 6 to 8 servings.

APPLE KUCHEN: Make Kuchen as above, omitting vanilla-wafer crumbs, but sprinkling dough with combined cinnamon, sugar and nutmeg. Substitute 3½ *cups thinly peeled and sliced apples* for 2 cups seedless grapes.

STRAWBERRY PYRAMID

2 10-ounce packages
frozen raspberries, thawed
1½ tablespoons cornstarch
1 tablespoon lemon juice
2 quarts hulled fresh strawberries
1 cup seeded white grapes

L is for Low-calorie, high-taste-level desserts

About 3 hours before serving: In medium saucepan, heat raspberries. In small cup, combine cornstarch with ¼ cup water. Gradually stir into raspberries; bring to boiling and stir in lemon juice. Press hot mixture through sieve; cool; refrigerate.

In large serving bowl, heap strawberries and grapes; refrigerate.

Just before serving: Pour some of raspberry sauce over berries; serve rest of sauce in pitcher. Makes 10 to 12 servings.

PINEAPPLE FRAPPÉ

Just before serving: Drain *one 30-ounce can pineapple chunks.* In covered electric-blender container, at high speed, blend pineapple, *1½ cups chopped ice and ⅛ to ¼ teaspoon mint extract.* Blend just until large chunks of ice disappear. Serve immediately in chilled dessert dishes. Makes 6 servings.

VERY-BERRY COMPOTE

3 pints strawberries, halved
½ cup granulated sugar
1 cup raspberries
1 cup blueberries
1½ pints vanilla ice cream, softened
2 tablespoons grated orange peel

About 2½ hours before serving: In large bowl, gently toss strawberries with granulated sugar; cover and refrigerate about 2 hours, tossing occasionally.

Just before serving: Alternately spoon strawberries, raspberries and blueberries into large glass bowl.

In medium bowl, combine ice cream with orange peel; spoon some on top of berries; pass any remaining ice cream in small bowl. Serve immediately. Makes 8 to 10 servings.

Baked Alaska, page 68, has no end of variations, as spectacular (and good) as the original

Peach Cake Roll, page 70, an old favorite, with peach pie filling

Baba au Rhum, **page** 77, a festive treat, soaked in rum syrup and glazed with jam

Peach Snow Mold, page 82, is a showy beauty that takes only minutes to make

Grape Delight, page 90, as easy to make as it is handsome to serve

Refrigerated rolls and frozen fruit combine into Quick Fruit Cobbler, **page** 91, in no time

Classic puff-pastry creations: Cream Horns; Cream-Filled Shells, page 98; Palmiers, page 97; Raspberry Puffs, page 96

An heirloom recipe to try and treasure, Apple Charlotte with Apricot Sauce, page 101

LEMON-BERRY RING

4 envelopes unflavored gelatin
¾ cup granulated sugar
1½ quarts buttermilk
1½ teaspoons grated lemon peel
7 tablespoons lemon juice
2 2-ounce envelopes whipped-topping mix
2 16-ounce packages
frozen whole strawberries, thawed
4 teaspoons cornstarch
red food color (optional)

Day before serving: In saucepan, combine gelatin and sugar; add buttermilk; mix well. Cook over medium heat, stirring constantly, until gelatin and sugar are just dissolved; stir in lemon peel and lemon juice. Refrigerate until slightly jellied.

With electric mixer, prepare whipped-topping mixes, in one bowl, as label directs. With same beaters, without washing, beat up gelatin mixture 30 seconds or until slightly bubbly; to it, add whipped topping; beat another 30 seconds or until creamy and smooth. Pour into 3-quart bundt cake pan; refrigerate.

About 45 minutes before serving: Drain syrup from berries into saucepan; warm over low heat. Meanwhile, stir 2 tablespoons cold water into cornstarch; gradually add to syrup; cook and stir until thickened. Add a few drops of red food color, if desired. Refrigerate until cool. Refrigerate drained berries.

To serve: Set bundt pan, just to rim, in warm water for 10 seconds. Lift from water; shake slightly to loosen gelatin. Unmold onto large, deep, round serving plate. Arrange drained strawberries on top of ring; pour syrup over them. Makes 10 servings.

CHUNKY FRUIT WHIP

2 cups applesauce
1 4½-ounce container
frozen whipped topping, thawed
1 tablespoon grated orange peel
4 oranges, peeled

About 20 minutes before serving: In medium bowl, combine applesauce and whipped topping. Fold orange peel into mixture. Cut oranges into bite-size pieces; reserve a few pieces for garnish; fold remaining pieces into mixture. (This will have a grainy texture.) Spoon into serving dishes; garnish with reserved orange pieces. Makes 8 servings.

PEACH SNOW MOLD
pictured between pages 80-81

⅓ cup granulated sugar
1 envelope unflavored gelatin
1¼ cups boiling water
3 egg whites, unbeaten
1 tablespoon grated lemon peel
1 tablespoon lemon juice
1 7¾-ounce jar junior-food peach puree

About 5 hours before serving: In small bowl, combine sugar and gelatin. Add boiling water, stirring until completely dissolved; let cool for ½ hour at room temperature.

In large bowl, combine egg whites and gelatin mixture. With electric mixer at high speed, beat until mixture has consistency of heavy cream. Fold in lemon peel, lemon juice and peach puree. Pour into 2-quart mold; refrigerate until firm, about 3 to 4 hours.

To serve: Dip mold, just to rim, quickly in and out of warm water. Shake mold gently to loosen gelatin. Unmold onto serving platter. Makes 8 servings.

WATERMELON ICE

½ small watermelon
3 tablespoons confectioners' sugar
1 tablespoon lemon juice
¼ teaspoon salt

Several days or day before serving: Remove seeds from watermelon and cut fruit into 6 cups chunks, about 1 inch square. In covered electric-blender container, at low speed, blend 1 cup chunks with sugar, lemon juice and salt until smooth; add remaining chunks and blend a few seconds until smooth. Pour into large shallow baking pan and place in freezer until partially frozen or mushy, about 2 hours.

Into chilled bowl, spoon watermelon mixture. With electric mixer at high speed, beat until fluffy. Pour into loaf pan and freeze until firm.

Before serving: Remove from freezer; let stand 10 minutes at room temperature before spooning into serving dishes. Makes five 1-cup servings.

◀§ CANTALOUPE ICE: Substitute 2 cantaloupes for watermelon; cut into enough chunks to make 6 cups; blend with ½ cup granulated sugar, 2 tablespoons lemon juice and ½ teaspoon salt until smooth. Freeze as above. Makes five 1-cup servings.

SUMMER TRIFLE

1 3¼-ounce package vanilla pudding-
and-pie filling
3 cups pineapple juice
½ teaspoon grated lemon peel
2 teaspoons ascorbic-acid mixture for fruit
4 peaches, peeled and sliced
2 cups purple grapes, halved and seeded
5 figs, sliced
1 pint strawberries

Early in day: In medium saucepan, place pudding; stir in juice; cook, stirring constantly, until smooth and thickened. Remove from heat and stir in lemon peel; cool.

Meanwhile, in medium bowl, mix ascorbic-acid mixture with 3 tablespoons water; toss well with peaches.

In serving bowl, layer fruits. Pour cooled pineapple pudding over them; refrigerate. Makes 8 servings.

CRÈME BARTLETT

6 egg yolks
3 cups skimmed milk
4 teaspoons grated orange peel
2 teaspoons granulated sugar
¼ teaspoon salt
1 teaspoon almond extract
2 29-ounce cans pear halves
1 30-ounce can fruit cocktail, drained

Early in day or at least 4 hours before serving: In medium saucepan, beat egg yolks slightly; gradually stir in skimmed milk. Over low heat, stirring constantly, cook egg mixture until mixture coats spoon, about ½ hour. Remove from heat; stir in orange peel, granulated sugar, salt and almond extract. Chill custard in refrigerator until just cool but not set.

Drain pear halves well on paper towels and arrange 2 pear halves in bottom of each of 8 sherbet dishes. Spoon custard over pears, then refrigerate.

At serving time: Top each dish with some of the well-chilled fruit cocktail. Makes 8 servings.

STRAWBERRY-MINT SHERBET RING

⅓ cup green crème de menthe
3 pints lemon sherbet
2 pints strawberries, hulled
shredded fresh, or canned flaked coconut

Early in day or day before: In large bowl, with electric mixer at medium speed, quickly combine crème de menthe and lemon sherbet. Pack into 5½-cup ring mold; freeze.

At serving time: Unmold sherbet by running small spatula around outside and inner edges of ring mold. Invert mold onto chilled serving plate; place cloth, wrung out in hot water, on top of it for a minute or two; then lift off mold. (If sherbet does not come out, repeat hot cloth treatment.)

Fill center of ring with strawberries; sprinkle lightly with coconut. Makes 8 to 10 servings.

FRUIT AND SHERBET COMPOTE

At least 1 hour before serving: Into large bowl, pour *1 cup orange juice;* into juice, slice *2 bananas.* Add *one 16-ounce can pineapple chunks* with *¼ cup syrup drained from pineapple* and *1 cup fresh or frozen fruits* such as strawberries, blueberries, sliced peaches and/or raspberries. Chill.

Just before serving: Top fruit with scoops of *lemon or lime sherbet.* Makes 6 to 8 servings.

FROSTED WATERMELON

½ watermelon
1 pint raspberry sherbet
1 pint fresh raspberries or 1 10-ounce package
frozen raspberries, thawed

Several hours ahead: With serving spoon, scoop meat from watermelon half in spoonfuls, reserving shell. With tip of paring knife, remove surface seeds from each spoonful of watermelon, then return watermelon to the shell with the rounded side up; refrigerate.

At serving time: Top watermelon with spoonfuls of raspberry sherbet; scatter raspberries over sherbet. Makes 16 servings.

BUTTERMILK-PINEAPPLE SHERBET
for crank-type freezer

2 envelopes unflavored gelatin
2 8½-ounce cans crushed pineapple
1 cup granulated sugar
1 quart buttermilk
¼ cup lemon juice
2 teaspoons vanilla extract

Several hours before churning: In medium saucepan, soften gelatin in syrup drained from pineapple; stir in sugar and heat until gelatin and sugar are dissolved. Pour into bowl; refrigerate until lukewarm.

Slowly stir buttermilk into lukewarm mixture; add juice, vanilla and pineapple. Chill 1 hour. Pour into freezer container and freeze according to manufacturer's directions. Makes 2 quarts or 16 servings.

RASPBERRY SHERBET PARFAIT

At serving time: Spoon one third of *1 pint raspberry sherbet* into 4 parfait or sherbet glasses; top with half *10-ounce package frozen raspberries,* thawed and drained. Sprinkle with *cinnamon.* Top with another third of the sherbet, then remaining raspberries. Add final layer of sherbet. Garnish with *fresh raspberries.* Makes 4 servings.

FRESH APPLE SNOW

4 large apples, peeled
1 teaspoon ascorbic-acid mixture for fruit
granulated sugar
3 tablespoons lemon juice
¼ teaspoon nutmeg
dash salt
2 egg whites
6 thin, unpeeled apple slices for garnish

Early in day: In covered electric-blender container or on grater, coarsely grate apples. In medium bowl, thoroughly mix ascorbic-acid mixture with 1½ tablespoons water; add grated apples, 2 tablespoons sugar, lemon juice, nutmeg and salt; refrigerate; stir occasionally.

Just before serving: In small bowl, with electric mixer at high speed, beat egg whites with ¼ cup sugar until soft peaks form. Drain apple mixture well; fold into egg whites; spoon into serving dishes; garnish with apple slices. Makes 6 servings.

CREAM-LEMON GINGER SQUARES

1 14- or 14.5-ounce package
gingerbread-cake mix
1 teaspoon instant coffee
1 teaspoon mace
1 teaspoon grated orange peel
½ cup orange juice
1 2-ounce package whipped-topping mix
1 8-ounce package cream cheese
¼ cup granulated sugar
3 tablespoons milk
1 3¼- or 3⅝-ounce package
lemon pudding-and-pie filling
1 tablespoon butter or margarine

*is for Mixes
for short-cut confections*

Early in day: Prepare and bake gingerbread mix as label directs, adding instant coffee, mace and orange peel, and using orange juice plus water for the liquid required.

Prepare topping mix as label directs. In bowl, with electric mixer at medium speed, beat cheese, sugar and milk until fluffy; fold in topping. Cover; chill.

In saucepan, bring lemon pudding and 3 cups water to boiling, stirring constantly, until slightly thickened. Remove from heat; add butter and stir until melted. Cover; chill.

To serve: Stir lemon sauce until smooth. Cut cake into 9 squares; top each square with spoonful of cheese topping and lemon sauce. Makes 9 servings. (Stir any leftover sauces together until smooth; spoon into sherbet dishes and refrigerate for dessert another day.)

PEANUT-BRITTLE CAKE

1 18.5-ounce package
orange-chiffon cake mix
2 2-ounce packages whipped-topping mix
1 teaspoon almond extract
½ pound peanut brittle

Day before serving: Prepare cake mix as label directs; store.

Up to 2 hours before dinner: Prepare topping mixes as label directs, substituting almond extract for vanilla.

On large cake plate, lay four 2-inch-wide waxed-paper strips to form a square. Set cake on top; frost with topping mix; remove paper.

With rolling pin, crush peanut brittle between sheets of waxed paper; sprinkle over cake; refrigerate. Makes 10 to 12 servings.

STRAWBERRY SHORTCAKE

¼ cup orange juice
1 teaspoon cornstarch
1 14- to 16-ounce package
frozen whole unsweetened strawberries,
partially thawed
⅓ cup granulated sugar
2 packaged 6-inch spongecake layers
1 cup frozen whipped topping, thawed

Early in day: Gradually blend orange juice into cornstarch. Stir until smooth. In saucepan, combine strawberries and sugar; over medium heat, bring to boiling; add orange-juice mixture. Cook, stirring, until slightly thickened. Cool; refrigerate.

About ½ hour before serving: On cake plate, place one of the cake layers; top with some of the berry mixture, then with remaining cake layer. Cover with whipped topping. Cut cake into 8 wedges. Serve each wedge topped with berry mixture. Makes 8 servings.

OLD-FASHIONED STRAWBERRY SHORTCAKE

2⅓ cups packaged buttermilk-biscuit mix
5 tablespoons granulated sugar
3 tablespoons melted butter
or margarine, cooled
½ cup milk
2 pints strawberries
1 2-ounce package whipped-topping mix
butter or margarine, softened

About 1 hour before serving: Preheat oven to 450° F. Grease one 8-inch layer-cake pan; line with waxed paper.

In bowl, combine biscuit mix, 3 tablespoons of the sugar, butter and milk. With fork, mix to soften dough. Roll or pat to fit pan. Bake 15 to 20 minutes or until golden. Remove from pan; cool on rack.

Meanwhile, wash and hull berries; reserve 9 for garnish. Into bowl, slice remaining berries; add remaining 2 tablespoons sugar. Prepare whipped topping as label directs. Split shortcake into 2 layers; on cake plate, place bottom half; spread with butter; cover with sliced strawberries, then top layer.

Cover with whipped topping and garnish with reserved whole strawberries. Makes 8 servings.

ALMOND TWISTS

1 8-ounce package refrigerated
crescent dinner rolls
1 egg, beaten
1 tablespoon granulated sugar
2½ teaspoons milk
2 teaspoons butter or margarine, softened
⅛ teaspoon almond extract
½ cup confectioners' sugar

About 45 minutes before serving: Preheat oven to 375° F. Unroll crescent dough and cut each piece in half along straight perforations; with fingers, press diagonal perforations together on all pieces. Cut each rectangle lengthwise into 6 strips. Twist 2 strips together like a rope; cut each rope in half.

On greased cookie sheet, place ropes about one inch apart; brush strips with egg and sprinkle with granulated sugar. Bake for 8 to 12 minutes or until golden.

In small bowl, blend milk, butter, almond extract and confectioners' sugar until smooth. Frost twists generously as soon as they come from oven. Serve hot. Makes 24.

CHERRY CLOUD

1 18½-ounce package white-cake mix
1 envelope unflavored gelatin
⅓ cup granulated sugar
⅛ teaspoon salt
1 cup boiling water
1 2-ounce package whipped-topping mix
2 16-ounce cans pitted red cherries,
drained

About 4 hours before serving: Prepare cake mix as label directs; bake in two 9-inch layer-cake pans. Cool on rack.

In bowl, over ½ cup cold water, sprinkle gelatin to soften. Add sugar, salt and 1 cup boiling water, stirring until thoroughly dissolved. Refrigerate until slightly thickened.

Prepare topping mix as label directs; gradually beat in gelatin.

On serving plate, place one of the cake layers; top with 1 of the cans of cherries; spread with 1 cup of the topping mixture. Top with second cake layer, then with remaining can of cherries; spread with topping mixture. Refrigerate 2 hours. Makes 10 to 12 servings.

QUICK CINNAMON ROLL

1 egg
2½ cups packaged buttermilk-biscuit mix
⅓ cup milk
2 tablespoons butter or margarine, softened
¼ cup granulated sugar
2 teaspoons cinnamon
3 tablespoons chopped citron
3 tablespoons chopped candied red cherries
¼ cup confectioners' sugar

Early in day: Preheat oven to 400° F. In medium bowl, beat egg lightly with fork. Add biscuit mix and milk, stirring with fork to a soft dough. Turn onto lightly floured surface and, with floured hands, knead lightly just until smooth.

With lightly floured rolling pin, roll dough into 10" by 8" rectangle. Spread with butter; sprinkle evenly with sugar, cinnamon, 2 tablespoons each of citron and cherries. Beginning at wide side, roll dough up tightly, jelly-roll fashion.

Place, seam side down, on ungreased cookie sheet. With scissors, cut roll almost through at one-inch intervals. Bake about 20 minutes or until lightly browned.

In small bowl, combine confectioners' sugar and 1½ teaspoons water; spread mixture evenly on warm roll; sprinkle top of roll with remaining citron and cherries. Remove to rack to cool. Makes 10 servings.

GOLDEN PEAR DESSERT

1 29-ounce can pear halves, drained
½ cup apricot preserves
1 2-ounce package whipped-topping mix
1 9-inch yellow-cake layer
slivered toasted almonds
halved strawberries (optional)

About 15 minutes before serving: Place pear halves on paper towels to dry, then arrange, rounded side up, on waxed paper.

In saucepan over low heat, melt apricot preserves; spoon over pear halves, coating them completely.

Prepare topping mix as label directs; spread over top and sides of cake. Arrange pears, spoke-fashion, on top of cake. Cover cake sides with toasted almonds. If desired, garnish with strawberries. Makes 12 servings.

GRAPE DELIGHT
pictured between pages 80-81

2 8¾-ounce cans seedless grapes, chilled
2 cups sour cream or yogurt
2 teaspoons grated orange peel
2 teaspoons orange juice
1 1-ounce square semisweet chocolate

About ½ hour before serving: Drain grapes. Combine sour cream, orange peel and juice. Into each of 4 glasses, spoon ¼ cup of the sour-cream mixture; top with ¼ cup grapes and then another ¼ cup sour cream.

Using vegetable peeler, shave some chocolate curls over each dessert. Refrigerate. Makes 4 servings.

FRUIT TORTE

½ 18-ounce roll refrigerated
sugar slice-and-bake cookie dough
4 eggs, separated
2 teaspoons grated lemon peel
½ cup lemon juice
granulated sugar
1 pint fresh strawberries, washed, halved
¼ teaspoon salt

About 1½ hours before serving: Let cookie dough soften at room temperature 5 to 10 minutes. Preheat oven to 375° F.

On lightly floured surface, with stockinette-covered rolling pin, roll cookie dough into 10″ by 9″ rectangle; with knife, trim edges even; bake on ungreased cookie sheet 10 minutes or until done. With spatula, remove cookie to board or rack; cool.

Meanwhile, in double-boiler top, beat egg yolks until thick. Stir in lemon peel and juice and ¼ cup sugar. Cook over boiling water, stirring, until thickened; cool; fold in strawberries. Return cookie to cookie sheet; spread with lemon-strawberry mixture.

Preheat oven to 425° F. In bowl, with electric mixer at high speed, beat egg whites and salt until foamy; gradually add ¼ cup sugar, beating until meringue is stiff and glossy. Spoon over lemon-strawberry mixture; bake 4 minutes or until browned. Cool on rack, away from draft. To serve, dip sharp knife into hot water; dry; slice torte crosswise. Makes 9 servings.

QUICK FRUIT COBBLER
pictured between pages 80-81

2 10-ounce packages frozen mixed fruit, thawed
2 tablespoons granulated sugar
2 tablespoons cornstarch
1 tablespoon lemon juice
½ teaspoon salt
1 9½-ounce package refrigerated
cinnamon rolls

About ½ hour before serving: Preheat oven to 375° F. In saucepan over medium heat, heat fruit, sugar, cornstarch, lemon juice and salt, stirring constantly, just until thickened. Pour mixture into 8-inch square baking dish. Arrange cinnamon rolls in one layer over fruits; reserve icing from package. Bake 20 minutes or until golden brown. Spread icing evenly on top of rolls. Serve hot. Makes 8 servings.

FRENCH APPLE TART

About 1 hour before serving: Preheat oven to 425° F. Onto cookie sheet, unroll *one roll of dough from package of refrigerated apple-turnover pastries;* overlap serrated cuts ¼ inch; press together. Repeat with second roll. Bake 8 to 10 minutes or to a rich brown. Cool on rack.

At serving time: Blend *one 3-ounce package cream cheese with 3 tablespoons milk* until smooth.

Spread the two pastry strips with cream cheese, then apple filling; sprinkle with nutmeg. (Save creamy icing to top breakfast toast; sprinkle with cinnamon.) Makes 8 servings.

CHOCOLATE BRANDY CAKE

3 2-ounce packages whipped-topping mix
3 tablespoons brandy extract
1 8½-ounce package round chocolate wafers

Day before: Line 9″ by 5″ loaf pan with waxed paper. Prepare topping mix as label directs, substituting brandy extract for vanilla. Quickly dip 1 wafer in water; lay in bottom of pan with 2 more wafers quickly dipped in water. Cover with thin layer of topping. Repeat layers, using all the topping and most of the wafers. Refrigerate.

To serve: Loosen cake, unmold; slice thickly. Makes about 10 servings.

LEMON SURPRISE

1 3¼-ounce package lemon
pudding-and-pie filling
granulated sugar
2 eggs, separated
7 packaged ladyfingers
2 tablespoons currant jelly
2 tablespoons graham-cracker crumbs (optional)

About 4 hours before serving: In saucepan, blend lemon pudding and ⅓ cup granulated sugar with ¼ cup cold water. Stir in egg yolks and 2 cups cold water; cook as pudding label directs.

Beat egg whites until foamy; add ¼ cup granulated sugar, one tablespoon at a time, beating well after each addition. Continue beating until stiff peaks are formed; gradually fold in pudding.

Line bottom of 8-inch square baking dish with split ladyfingers. Spread ladyfingers with jelly; top with pudding mixture and sprinkle with graham cracker crumbs. Refrigerate 3 hours. Makes 9 servings.

LEMON PETAL DELIGHT

1 16-ounce roll refrigerated fudge-nut
slice-and-bake cookie dough
1 3½-ounce package lemon-flavor
whipped-dessert mix
1 6-ounce can frozen limeade concentrate,
diluted
¼ cup whipped-dessert topping
chocolate sprinkles

Several hours before serving: Preheat oven to 350° F. Between 2 pieces of waxed paper, with rolling pin, roll ¼ of the cookie dough into a circle ⅛ inch thick. Transfer circle to greased 9-inch pie plate; with paring knife, trim it to fit bottom of plate.

With sharp knife, from rest of roll of cookie dough, cut 12 to 14 very thin slices. Arrange around inside of pie plate, just touching, to line sides; bend tops over to cover pie-plate rim. Bake 10 minutes; cool on rack.

Meanwhile, prepare whipped-dessert mix as label directs, substituting 1 cup of the diluted limeade for milk and water. Spoon into cooled cookie shell. Refrigerate until ready to serve.

To serve: Just before serving, garnish pie with whipped topping and chocolate sprinkles. Cut into wedges. Makes 8 servings.

FRUIT PINWHEELS

Early in day: Preheat oven to 400° F. Remove dough from *one package refrigerated cherry, blueberry* or *apple turnovers;* refrigerate half of dough. Separate other half into its squares.

On lightly floured surface, roll one square into 5-inch square; cut into quarters. Place one quarter on cookie sheet. Slit it from each corner to ½ inch of center. In center, place ½ teaspoon filling from turnover package; bring every other corner to center to make pinwheel. Repeat with other 3 quarters. Roll, quarter and shape remaining dough, as well as refrigerated portion, in same way.

Bake pinwheels 5 minutes, or until golden. Remove to racks to cool. If desired, glaze with your favorite frosting. Makes 32 pinwheels.

NUTTED ICE-CREAM CAKE

1 cup evaporated milk
dash salt
1 12-ounce package semisweet-chocolate
pieces (2 cups)
2 teaspoons vanilla extract
9 packaged frozen waffles
½-gallon rectangular package
vanilla ice cream
¾ cup chopped walnuts

Up to 3 days before serving: In small saucepan over medium heat, bring milk and salt to boiling, stirring constantly. Remove from heat; add chocolate pieces and vanilla; stir until a smooth glaze.

Using tongs, dip unthawed waffles, one at a time, in glaze, removing any excess with pastry brush. Lay waffles flat on rack. With pastry brush, touch up marks left by tongs on top of waffles; place in freezer.

Remove ice cream from package; trim to block about 7″ by 3½″ by 2¾″ (same size as waffles). (Freeze excess ice cream for later use.) With broad side up, sprinkle top of ice-cream block only with ⅓ cup of the walnuts, pressing them in lightly. Cut block into eight 3½″ by 2¾″ slices; place slices, not touching, on cookie sheet. Freeze.

About 5 hours before serving: Refrigerate a cookie sheet ½ hour.

Remove ice-cream slices and waffles from freezer. With broad spatula, loosen ice-cream slices. On chilled cookie sheet, starting with a waffle, alternate waffles, long side up, and ice-cream slices, walnut-side up, in a row. Press row together lightly. Freeze.

To serve: Transfer ice-cream cake to platter; let stand 10 minutes to soften slightly. Serve at table, slicing off a waffle-and-ice-cream section for each serving; sprinkle with rest of nuts. Makes 8 servings.

RICE CHANTILLY

1 3¼-ounce package vanilla
pudding-and-pie filling
dash salt
⅓ cup packaged precooked rice
½ cup heavy or whipping cream, whipped
2 tablespoons confectioners' sugar
½ teaspoon vanilla extract
nutmeg

Several hours before serving: In saucepan, prepare vanilla pudding as label directs, adding salt and rice. Pour into large bowl and place waxed paper directly on surface of pudding to prevent "skin" forming; refrigerate.

Into cooled pudding mixture, fold whipped cream, sugar and vanilla. Spoon into 6 sherbet glasses; sprinkle with nutmeg. Refrigerate until serving time. Also nice spooned over fruit. Makes 6 servings.

CHERRY PINWHEELS

1 16-ounce can pitted red cherries
in heavy syrup
4 teaspoons all-purpose flour
1 8-ounce can refrigerated
crescent dinner rolls
butter or margarine, softened
1 tablespoon cornstarch
1 tablespoon red cinnamon-candy drops
vanilla ice cream

About 45 minutes before serving: Preheat oven to 450° F. Drain cherries; reserve syrup. Dry cherries on paper towels; sprinkle with flour, then toss to coat evenly.

Unroll dough; spread the 2 strips lightly with 2 tablespoons butter; top with cherries. Roll up jelly-roll fashion. Cut each roll into 3 crosswise slices; place, cut side down, in greased jelly-roll pan. Bake 15 to 18 minutes or until done.

Meanwhile, in saucepan, blend cornstarch with a bit of cherry syrup; stir in remaining syrup and cinnamon candy. Cook over low heat, stirring, until clear and thickened.

Brush baked pinwheels with 2 tablespoons butter. Serve warm, topped with the hot sauce and a bit of ice cream. Makes 6 servings.

NO-BAKE MARBLED CHEESECAKE

1⅓ cups graham-cracker crumbs
or vanilla-wafer crumbs
2¼ cups granulated sugar
¼ cup melted butter or margarine
1 envelope unflavored gelatin
1 4-ounce package chocolate-flavor
whipped-dessert mix
3 8-ounce packages cream cheese, softened
⅛ teaspoon cinnamon
1 3½-ounce package vanilla-flavor
whipped-dessert mix
grated peel of 1 lemon

Day before or early in day: In bowl, combine crumbs, ¼ cup of the sugar and melted butter. Press mixture firmly into bottom of 9- or 10-inch springform pan.

In measuring cup, sprinkle gelatin over ¼ cup cold water; place cup in small saucepan of hot water over medium heat and stir until gelatin is dissolved.

Prepare chocolate whipped-dessert mix as label directs; set aside.

In large bowl, with electric mixer at medium speed, beat 1½ packages of the cream cheese and 1 cup of the sugar until smooth; beat in chocolate mixture along with 2 tablespoons of the dissolved gelatin and cinnamon until just blended; set aside. Quickly prepare vanilla whipped-dessert mix as label directs; set aside.

In large bowl, with electric mixer at medium speed, beat remaining cream cheese and remaining 1 cup sugar until smooth; beat in vanilla mixture along with remaining dissolved gelatin and grated lemon peel until just blended. Using two large spoons, alternately drop chocolate and vanilla mixtures evenly onto crumb crust. Using tip of knife, lightly score top surface in crisscross pattern. Refrigerate until firm, at least 6 hours.

To serve: With spatula, loosen edge of cheesecake from pan; carefully remove sides of springform pan. Makes 14 to 16 servings.

FRUITED RICE PUDDING

About 1 hour before serving: Drain one 8¾-ounce can apricot halves, reserving liquid. Dice apricots, reserving 6 pieces for garnish. In large bowl, combine *two 7-ounce cans ready-to-serve rice pudding* with reserved apricot liquid, diced apricots and ¼ teaspoon nutmeg. Spoon rice mixture into 5 or 6 parfait glasses and garnish with reserved fruit. Chill until serving time. Makes 5 or 6 servings.

PETITS NAPOLEONS

1 3¼-ounce package vanilla
pudding-and-pie filling
1 cup skimmed milk
½ teaspoon rum extract
1 10-ounce package piecrust mix
½ cup whipped topping
½ cup confectioners' sugar
1 1-ounce square semisweet chocolate
2 tablespoons light corn syrup

is for Napoleons and their puff-pastry kin

Early in day: Prepare pudding as label directs, using only 1 cup skimmed milk and adding rum extract. Pour into small bowl; lay piece of waxed paper directly on warm pudding; refrigerate until cold.

Preheat oven to 425° F. Prepare piecrust as label directs; roll into 14" by 10" rectangle. Cut pastry rectangle into 3 strips, each about 14" by 3⅓"; lift strips onto ungreased cookie sheet; prick well with fork; bake 12 minutes or until golden. Cool on rack.

Three hours before serving: With electric mixer, beat pudding about 10 minutes or until light and fluffy; fold in whipped topping. On each of two pastry strips, spread ¾ cup pudding; on cutting board, stack them, one on top of the other. Next, in small bowl, stir confectioners' sugar with 1 tablespoon water until smooth; using pastry brush, spread over third pastry strip. In double boiler, over hot, *not boiling*, water, melt chocolate; stir in corn syrup and 1½ teaspoons water; remove from heat. While icing is still moist, lightly draw tip of knife, dipped in melted chocolate, lengthwise through icing in zigzag pattern. Set iced strip on top of others; refrigerate 2½ to 3 hours.

To serve: Using very sharp knife, in sawing motion, cut strip into thirds, crosswise, then cut each third into thirds. Makes 9 servings.

RASPBERRY PUFFS
pictured between pages 80-81

Early in day: Preheat oven to 450° F. On floured surface, roll out ¼ of *Puff Pastry* (opposite) ¼ inch thick. Cut into 2-inch rounds; with one light stroke of rolling pin, form each into an oval. With ½-inch cookie cutter, cut almost, but not quite, through center of each round. On brown-paper-lined cookie sheet, 2½ inches apart, place ovals. Bake 5 minutes, then every 5 minutes reduce oven heat 50° F., until ovals are puffed and golden, about 15 minutes. Cool on rack.

With sharp knife, remove centers of puffs, along with a bit of the pastry underneath; sprinkle puffs with *confectioners' sugar*, then fill centers with *raspberry jam*. Makes about 8 puffs.

PUFF PASTRY

1 cup ice water
3½ cups all-purpose flour,
sifted before measuring
2 cups butter, softened

Several days before serving or early in day: In large bowl, add ice water
to flour; with fork, mix thoroughly until dough is stiff. Knead dough in
bowl 5 minutes, then turn out on lightly floured surface; cover with bowl
and let dough rest 15 minutes.

Roll dough into rectangle ¼ inch thick; starting at edge, spread
two-thirds of dough with ½ cup of the butter. Fold unbuttered third of
dough over middle third; cover with last buttered third, making 3 layers
with all edges meeting exactly. This completes the first "turn." Repeat
this turn with another ½ cup butter. Wrap dough in waxed paper; place
in freezer 10 minutes. Repeat turn two more times, using ½ cup butter
Several days before serving or early in day: In large bowl, add ice water
each time. Now roll and fold it twice more, omitting butter, for a total of
6 turns. Wrap in foil; refrigerate for several hours, or freeze for up to
one month. Use dough (if frozen, thaw for 2 hours at room temperature,
or overnight in the refrigerator) to make Palmiers, Raspberry Puffs,
Cream Horns and Cream-Filled Shells.

ᐁ§ EASY PUFF PASTRY: Thaw *one 10-ounce package frozen patty
shells* at room temperature for about 1 hour. Press shells together to
form rectangle. Roll out and proceed as directed above.

PALMIERS
pictured between pages 80-81

¼ of Puff Pastry (above)
1 egg white
granulated sugar
1 cup Cream Chantilly (page 98),
optional

About 3 hours before serving: Preheat oven to 425° F. On lightly floured
surface, roll dough into 12″ by 8″ rectangle. Trim edges straight; brush
with slightly beaten egg white; sprinkle with ¼ cup sugar. Fold 12-inch
sides of dough to meet in middle; sprinkle with 1 tablespoon sugar; fold
in half to form a long narrow strip. Cut into ¼-inch slices; place, cut
side down, on cookie sheet; press lightly to flatten. Bake 8 minutes; turn
over; bake 4 minutes more. Cool on rack.

Just before serving: If desired, sandwich 10 pairs of Palmiers together
with Cream Chantilly. Makes 10 servings.

CREAM HORNS
pictured between pages 80-81

¼ of Puff Pastry (page 97)
1 egg white
1 cup Cream Chantilly (below)
3 tablespoons raspberry jam
chopped nuts or chocolate curls

About 3 hours before serving: Preheat oven to 450° F. On lightly floured surface, roll dough into 12″ by 10″ rectangle. Cut into 9 strips, 12 inches long. Wrap each strip around a greased metal cone, starting at pointed end and letting each strip overlap the preceding one. Pinch the end firmly to cone to anchor it; place, pinched end down, on greased cookie sheet. Brush with slightly beaten egg white. Bake 10 minutes; remove cones; bake 3 to 4 minutes longer. Cool on rack.

Just before serving: Fill each pastry cone with 1 teaspoon of the jam. With rosette or star tube, pipe Cream Chantilly into cones. Garnish with nuts or chocolate curls. Makes 9 servings.

CREAM CHANTILLY

Just before serving: In small mixing bowl, with electric mixer at medium speed, beat *1 cup heavy* or *whipping cream* until thick. Fold in ¼ *teaspoon vanilla extract* and *4 teaspoons granulated sugar*. Use to fill Cream Horns and Palmiers. Makes 2 cups.

CREAM-FILLED SHELLS
pictured between pages 80-81

Early in day: Prepare one 3¼-ounce *package vanilla-* or one 3¾-ounce *package chocolate-pudding-and-pie filling* as label directs, but use only 1½ *cups milk*. Pour into bowl; stir in ¼ *cup rum;* lay waxed paper directly on surface of pudding; chill.

Preheat oven to 450° F. On floured surface, roll out ¼ of *Puff Pastry* (page 97) ⅜ inch thick; cut into 2¾-inch rounds. Bake on brown-paper-lined cookie sheet 10 minutes, then every 5 minutes reduce oven heat 50° F. until puffs are round and golden, about ½ hour. Cool on rack.

About 1 hour before serving: Whip ½ *cup heavy* or *whipping cream;* beat pudding until smooth; fold in whipped cream. With sharp knife, split pastry shells into 2 or 3 layers; spread filling between layers. Garnish with *whipped cream* if desired. Refrigerate until serving time, along with leftover filling (serve as pudding later). Makes 8.

MARY'S FUDGE PUDDING

1 cup all-purpose flour,
sifted before measuring
1½ teaspoons baking powder
salt
¼ cup butter or margarine, softened
granulated sugar
½ cup milk
1 1-ounce square unsweetened chocolate, melted
1 teaspoon vanilla extract
¾ cup coarsely chopped nuts
½ cup packed brown sugar
3 tablespoons cocoa
1½ cups boiling water

is for Oven treats, fragrant and warm

About 1½ hours before serving: Preheat oven to 350° F. Sift flour with baking powder and ½ teaspoon salt. In bowl, with spoon, cream butter with ⅔ cup granulated sugar until light and fluffy. Add flour mixture with milk, stirring just enough to blend. Add chocolate, vanilla and nuts; turn into 8-inch square pan.

Combine brown sugar with ½ cup granulated sugar, cocoa and ¼ teaspoon salt; sprinkle over batter. Pour boiling water over batter; don't stir.

Bake 1 hour (pudding will separate into cake and sauce layers) . Cool slightly in pan.

Serve warm, cut into squares, topped with sauce spooned from bottom of pan. Pass cream if desired. Makes 9 servings.

PEAR-BUTTERSCOTCH CRISP

1 29-ounce can pear halves, drained
½ cup all-purpose flour
¼ teaspoon salt
½ cup packed brown sugar
¼ teaspoon cinnamon
¼ cup butter or margarine

About 1 hour before serving: Preheat oven to 425° F. In greased pie plate, arrange pear halves, cut sides down. In small bowl, combine flour, salt, brown sugar and cinnamon; with fork or pastry blender, work in butter until crumbly. Sprinkle thickly over and around pears. Bake 15 to 20 minutes or until crumbs are golden brown. Serve warm, with ice cream or chilled custard if desired. Makes 4 servings.

BUTTERSCOTCH PEARS

2 29-ounce cans pear halves
2 cups packaged bite-size shredded-rice cereal
butter or margarine, softened
½ teaspoon salt
¾ cup packed light brown sugar
½ teaspoon nutmeg
cream (optional)

About ½ hour before serving: Drain pears, reserving syrup. Chill. Lightly grease 9-inch pie plate. Preheat oven to 425° F.

In large bowl, with two forks or serving spoons, toss cereal with 5 tablespoons butter, salt, sugar and nutmeg until well mixed.

Sprinkle some of the cereal mixture over bottom and sides of pie plate. Place layer of pears in bottom of plate; sprinkle with some of cereal mixture. Repeat layers, heaping pears in center of plate. Sprinkle remaining cereal over the top of pears.

Bake 8 to 10 minutes or until pears are hot. Serve warm with the reserved syrup and/or cream, if desired. Makes 8 to 10 servings.

BANANA-COCONUT BETTY

⅓ cup melted butter or margarine
2 cups fresh bread crumbs
4 bananas, thinly sliced
⅓ cup granulated sugar
½ teaspoon nutmeg
½ teaspoon cinnamon
1 tablespoon grated lemon peel
3 tablespoons lemon juice
½ cup flaked coconut

About 1 hour before serving: Preheat oven to 375° F. Toss butter with bread crumbs. In greased 1½-quart casserole, arrange one third of this mixture. Cover with half of bananas and half of combined sugar, nutmeg, cinnamon and lemon peel. Cover with one third of crumbs, rest of bananas and rest of sugar mixture.

Combine lemon juice and ¼ cup water; spoon on fruit. Combine remaining crumbs and coconut; use to top mixture. Bake, covered, ½ hour. Uncover; bake 5 to 10 minutes longer or until coconut mixture is golden.

Serve warm, with pour cream or whipped cream sprinkled with cinnamon, if desired. Makes 6 servings.

APPLE CHARLOTTE WITH APRICOT SAUCE
pictured between pages 80-81

14 medium McIntosh apples,
peeled, cored and quartered
butter or margarine
½ cup red cinnamon candy drops
1 teaspoon grated lemon peel
4 slices white bread
1 12-ounce jar apricot jam
2 tablespoons cornstarch

Early in day: In large, heavy saucepan, place apples; add 3 tablespoons butter, cinnamon drops and lemon peel. Cover; cook over low heat, stirring occasionally, 10 to 15 minutes or until apples can be pierced with two-tined fork. Cover; refrigerate.

About 1 hour before serving: Preheat oven to 425° F. Butter 1½-quart ovenproof bowl. Cut bread slices in half from corner to corner, making 8 triangles. Spread one side of each triangle with softened butter. Line bottom of bowl with 4 triangles, buttered side against bowl. Fit remaining triangles around sides, buttered sides against bowl. Fill bread shell with drained, cooled apples, pressing down firmly. Bake ½ hour.

Meanwhile, make apricot sauce: In saucepan, combine jam and ¼ cup water; bring to boiling; stirring constantly, cook over low heat for about 5 minutes. Blend cornstarch with 2 tablespoons of cold water until smooth; stir into sauce; cook, stirring constantly, until thickened.

As soon as charlotte is done, with spatula, loosen sides from bowl; unmold onto serving plate. Drizzle apricot sauce over top and down sides of charlotte. Serve warm, cut into wedges. Makes 8 servings.

HURRY-UP APPLE "PIE"

1 cup packaged piecrust mix
½ teaspoon nutmeg
½ cup packed brown sugar
½ teaspoon cinnamon
1 16-ounce can applesauce (2 cups)
1 tablespoon lemon juice
light cream

About 1 hour before serving: Preheat oven to 375° F. Grease 8-inch pie plate. In bowl, combine piecrust mix, nutmeg, brown sugar and cinnamon until crumbly. Into pie plate, spoon applesauce; sprinkle with lemon juice, then spread with crumbly mixture. Bake 25 minutes or until bubbly. Serve warm, with cream. Makes 4 servings.

CRANBERRY-CRUNCH À LA MODE

1 cup uncooked rolled oats
½ cup all-purpose flour,
sifted before measuring
1 cup packed brown sugar
½ cup butter or margarine
1 16-ounce can jellied or whole
cranberry sauce
vanilla ice cream

About 1 hour before serving: Preheat oven to 350° F. Lightly grease 8-inch square pan. In bowl, combine oats, flour and sugar; with 2 knives used scissor-fashion, cut in butter until crumbly. Place half of crumb mixture in pan; cover with cranberry sauce; top with remaining oat mixture. Bake 45 minutes. Serve hot, cut into squares and topped with ice cream. Makes 6 to 8 servings.

CINNAMON APPLE CHARLOTTE

3 large Rome Beauty apples
14 slices white bread
½ cup butter or margarine
½ cup packed dark brown sugar
½ teaspoon cinnamon
1 tablespoon light corn syrup

About 1½ hours before serving: Peel, core and slice apples to make approximately 6½ cups. In covered saucepan, cook apple slices in ½ cup water for 5 minutes or until fork-tender; drain; reserve 6 of prettiest slices.

Trim crusts from bread; tear as many crusts as needed to make 1 cup bread crumbs. In skillet, melt ¼ cup of the butter; add bread crumbs and sauté until crisp and golden. Remove from heat; stir in sugar and cinnamon. Preheat oven to 425° F.

Spread bread slices with remaining ¼ cup butter. In 1½-quart heatproof bowl, arrange 10 of the slices, buttered side to bowl, overlapping around sides. Use one slice, buttered side down, to cover bottom. Fill bowl with alternate layers of apples and crumbs, pressing down firmly. Trim remaining 3 bread slices to completely cover top, buttered sides up. Cover top of bowl with double thickness of foil; secure with string. Bake 1 hour. Remove string and foil; if bread is not golden, bake a few minutes longer. Loosen sides; unmold onto serving dish. In saucepan, gently heat reserved apple slices in corn syrup, then arrange on top of charlotte. Makes 6 servings.

EASY-DOES-IT APPLE DUMPLINGS

1 8-ounce can refrigerated
crescent dinner rolls
2 medium apples, peeled, cored
1 tablespoon granulated sugar
1 teaspoon cinnamon
¼ cup melted butter or margarine
¼ cup apricot jam
1 tablespoon butter or margarine
¼ teaspoon nutmeg

About 1 hour before serving: Preheat oven to 400° F. Separate refrigerated dough into 8 triangles. Halve apples. Combine sugar and cinnamon.

Place 2 of the dough triangles, with short sides touching, on greased
jelly-roll pan; brush with some of the melted butter. Place half an apple,
cut side down, in center of the 2 triangles; sprinkle with 1 teaspoon of
sugar-cinnamon mixture. Fold end of 1 triangle over apple at right angle,
forming another triangle. Fold end of other triangle over apple in same
way, forming square with bit of apple showing down the center. Repeat
with remaining apple halves and triangles to make 4 dumplings in all.
Bake 20 minutes or until apples are tender; brush with remaining butter.

Meanwhile, in small saucepan, heat jam with 3 tablespoons water, 1
tablespoon butter and nutmeg, stirring until smooth.

To serve: Spoon apricot mixture over warm dumplings. Makes 4
servings.

OLD-FASHIONED PEACH DUMPLINGS

pastry for 9-inch two-crust pie
6 ripe peaches, peeled
2 tablespoons currant jelly
granulated sugar
1 cup hot water
2 tablespoons butter or margarine
1 tablespoon grated lemon peel
3 tablespoons lemon juice
1 egg white

About 2 hours before serving: Roll pastry ⅛ inch thick; cut into six 7-
inch squares. Halve and pit peaches. Place peach half in center of each
pastry square; fill each hollow with 1 teaspoon of the currant jelly; top
with second peach half; sprinkle each with 2 tablespoons sugar. Moisten
edges of squares with cold water; bring points up over peaches; press

edges together. Place in well-greased 12″ by 8″ baking dish.

Preheat oven to 375° F. Combine hot water with ¼ cup granulated sugar, butter and grated lemon peel and juice; heat until sugar dissolves; pour into dumpling baking dish. Brush dumplings with slightly beaten egg white; sprinkle with sugar. Bake 40 minutes or until tender.

Serve warm, with pour cream; whipped cream; Lemon Sauce (page 124) or Ice-Cream Sauce (page 125). Makes 6 servings.

◆§ APPLE DUMPLINGS: *Use 6 peeled, cored, medium cooking apples (save peelings) instead of peaches. Instead of jelly, mix ½ cup granulated sugar with 1 teaspoon cinnamon; use to fill apples; dot each with bit of butter (1 tablespoon in all). Wrap in pastry, and place in baking dish as above; refrigerate.*

Pour 1½ cups boiling water over apple peelings; cover; simmer 20 minutes. Drain peelings; stir liquid with 2 tablespoons sugar, ¼ cup butter or margarine, ¼ teaspoon cinnamon, 1 tablespoon grated lemon peel and 3 tablespoons lemon juice until sugar dissolves. Pour into dumpling dish. Bake at 375° F. 40 minutes or until apples are tender. Makes 6 servings.

OLD-FASHIONED APPLE DUMPLINGS

pastry for 9-inch two-crust pie
1 cup granulated sugar
1 teaspoon cinnamon
4 large McIntosh apples
2 teaspoons butter or margarine
1 cinnamon stick
few drops red food color
1 egg yolk (optional)

About 1 hour before serving: Preheat oven to 425° F. Divide pastry into fourths; roll each into square. Mix ⅓ cup of the sugar with cinnamon.

Peel and core apples; center an apple on each pastry square. Fill cavities of apples with cinnamon-and-sugar mixture. Dot pastry with butter. Moisten points of each pastry square, then bring points up over apple, overlapping them, and sealing well all around apple. Place in four individual 10-, 15- or 16-ounce baking dishes, or slightly separated in a 12″ by 8″ baking dish.

Make syrup by boiling remaining sugar with cinnamon stick and 1⅓ cups water 3 minutes; remove cinnamon stick; add food color, a drop at a time, until syrup is of desired color; pour syrup around dumplings; brush tops of dumplings with slightly beaten egg yolk, if desired. Bake 40 to 45 minutes, or until crust is brown. Serve warm, as is, or topped with light cream or vanilla ice cream. Makes 4 servings.

CARAMEL APPLE DUMPLINGS

1 10-ounce package piecrust mix
3 medium baking apples
1 egg, beaten
½ cup caramel topping (from jar)
2 tablespoons butter or margarine
⅓ cup packed dark brown sugar
¼ cup toasted, slivered almonds

About 2 hours before serving: Prepare piecrust mix as label directs. On floured surface, roll three-fourths of the pastry into rectangle 22″ by 8″; with fluted pastry wheel, cut rectangle into three 7-inch squares. Roll remaining fourth, with any scraps, to ⅛ inch thickness; with pastry wheel, cut into six 6″ by ¾″ strips, and three 1-inch circles. Preheat oven to 350° F.

Peel and core apples. Place an apple on each 7-inch square; turn all 4 points of dough up to top of each apple, forming 4 "ears," pressing edges together lightly. Over each dumpling, lay two of the strips of dough, crosswise, and top with a pastry circle; brush with beaten egg; place in 12″ by 8″ baking dish. In small saucepan, combine caramel topping, butter and sugar with ¾ cup water; bring to boiling. Pour over dumplings. Bake 45 minutes or until apples are fork-tender, basting occasionally with caramel sauce.

To serve: Sprinkle with almonds. Serve half a dumpling, slightly cooled, with some sauce spooned over it. Makes 6 servings.

SUGAR-CRUSTED APPLES

⅔ cup granulated sugar
⅓ cup all-purpose flour
½ teaspoon cinnamon
⅓ cup butter or margarine
1 egg
6 large cooking apples, cored and peeled
¾ cup apple cider

About 1½ hours before serving: Preheat oven to 350° F. In bowl, mix sugar, flour and cinnamon; with fork or pastry blender, cut in butter.

In cup, beat egg slightly and brush on apples. Coat apples with sugar mixture; place in greased, shallow baking dish and fill centers with any remaining sugar mixture. Pour cider in bottom of dish. Bake 1 hour or until apples are just tender.

To serve: Spoon sauce from baking dish over apples. Makes 6 servings.

BAKED CHERRY TAPIOCA

1 16-ounce can pitted, red cherries,
undrained
1 tablespoon lemon juice
½ cup granulated sugar
1 teaspoon salt
dash nutmeg
⅓ cup quick-cooking tapioca
whipped cream or dessert topping

About 1 hour before serving: Preheat oven to 350° F. In 1-quart casserole, stir together cherries, ¾ cup hot water, lemon juice, sugar, salt, nutmeg and tapioca. Bake 35 minutes, stirring occasionally, or until tapioca granules are clear and pudding has thickened.

Serve warm with whipped cream or dessert topping. Makes 6 servings.

APPLE PANDOWDY

1 cup packed brown sugar
1¼ cups all-purpose flour,
sifted before measuring
1 teaspoon salt
1 teaspoon vinegar
2 teaspoons double-acting baking powder
3 tablespoons shortening
¾ cup milk
5 cups sliced, peeled, cored cooking apples
¼ teaspoon cinnamon
dash nutmeg
1 teaspoon lemon juice
1 teaspoon vanilla extract
2 tablespoons butter or margarine

About 1½ hours before serving: In saucepan, combine sugar with ¼ cup of the flour and ¼ teaspoon of the salt; stir in vinegar and 1 cup water; cook over low heat, stirring, until thickened. Set aside.

Preheat oven to 375° F. Sift remaining 1 cup flour and ¾ teaspoon salt with baking powder. With 2 knives used scissor-fashion, cut in shortening until size of peas; add milk; stir just until moistened.

Arrange apples in greased 12″ by 8″ baking dish. To brown sugar and water mixture, add cinnamon and remaining ingredients; pour over apples; cover with spoonfuls of dough. Bake 40 minutes or until golden.

Serve warm as is, or with cream or ice cream. Makes 6 servings.

CHERRY COFFEECAKE

1¾ cups all-purpose flour,
sifted before measuring
⅛ teaspoon salt
¼ teaspoon baking soda
1 teaspoon double-acting baking powder
½ cup shortening
¾ cup granulated sugar
1 egg
½ cup milk
2 tablespoons butter or margarine
¼ teaspoon cinnamon
1½ cups canned cherry-pie filling

Early in day: Preheat oven to 350° F. Grease and flour an 8-inch square pan. Sift 1¼ cups of the flour with salt, baking soda and baking powder.

In large bowl, with electric mixer at medium speed, beat shortening, ½ cup of the sugar and egg until light and fluffy. At low speed, beat in alternately flour mixture and milk until smooth. Pour into pan.

With fork, combine butter, remaining flour and sugar, and cinnamon. Sprinkle one-fourth of mixture over batter; cover with pie filling, then remaining topping. Bake 1 hour 15 minutes or until cake tester comes out clean. Serve warm, cut in squares. Makes 8 servings.

TOPAZ APPLE TAPIOCA

3 large apples, peeled,
cut into eighths
2 tablespoons butter or margarine
1 teaspoon mace
⅓ cup quick-cooking tapioca
1 cup packed light brown sugar
¾ teaspoon salt
2 tablespoons lemon juice
light cream

About 45 minutes before serving: Preheat oven to 375° F. Arrange apple slices, in even rows, in lightly greased, 9-inch square baking dish. Dot with butter and sprinkle with mace.

In saucepan, combine tapioca, brown sugar, salt, lemon juice and 2¼ cups water; bring to boiling, while stirring.

Pour hot tapioca mixture over apple slices; bake 20 minutes or until apple slices are fork-tender.

Serve hot or warm, with light cream. Makes 6 servings.

REGAL RHUBARB COBBLER

6 cups fresh rhubarb,
in ½-inch pieces
granulated sugar
¼ cup all-purpose flour
cinnamon
1 cup buttermilk-biscuit mix
1 tablespoon butter or margarine, softened
⅓ cup milk

About 2 hours before serving: Preheat oven to 425° F. In bowl, mix rhubarb with 1½ cups granulated sugar, flour and 1¼ teaspoons cinnamon; turn into greased 12″ by 8″ baking dish; add ¼ cup water.

In small bowl, combine biscuit mix, 1 tablespoon granulated sugar, ¼ teaspoon cinnamon, butter and milk, to make a soft dough. On floured surface, roll out to 13″ by 6″ rectangle. Cut into strips, ½ inch wide. Lay 3 of these strips, lengthwise, on top of rhubarb in baking dish; weave 4 pastry strips, cut to fit width of dish, into other pastry strips, as pictured. Bake ½ hour; cover with foil; bake 10 minutes longer.

Serve warm as is, or with vanilla ice cream. Makes 6 servings.

APPLE BROWN BETTY

⅓ cup melted butter or margarine
2 cups fresh bread crumbs
6 cups sliced, peeled, cored cooking apples
½ cup granulated or brown sugar
½ teaspoon nutmeg
1 tablespoon grated lemon peel
¼ teaspoon cinnamon
2 tablespoons lemon juice

About 1½ hours before serving: Preheat oven to 375° F. Toss butter with crumbs; arrange one third of crumbs in greased 1½-quart casserole. Cover with 3 cups of the apples and half of combined sugar, nutmeg, lemon peel and cinnamon. Add another one third of crumbs, then remaining apples and sugar mixture. Spoon on combined lemon juice and ¼ cup water; top with remaining crumbs. Cover; bake ½ hour. Uncover; bake ½ hour longer or until apples are done.

Serve warm as is, or topped with whipped cream sprinkled with cinnamon or shredded cheese; with cream cheese softened with a little milk; or ice cream. Makes 6 servings.

CREAMY BAKED RICE PUDDING

1 quart milk
¼ cup uncooked regular white rice*
¼ cup granulated sugar
1 tablespoon butter or margarine
¼ teaspoon salt
1 teaspoon vanilla extract
¼ teaspoon nutmeg
½ cup raisins, optional

About 3½ hours before serving: Preheat oven to 325° F. In greased 1½-quart casserole, combine milk, rice, sugar, butter, salt, vanilla and nutmeg. Bake, uncovered, stirring often, 2½ hours, or until rice is done. If desired, add raisins after first hour of baking.

Serve warm or cold, as is, or topped with cream, whipped cream, caramel sauce, fruit, berries or maple sugar. Makes 4 to 6 servings.

* For thicker pudding, increase rice to 5 tablespoons.

INDIAN PUDDING

1 quart milk
¼ cup cornmeal
¼ cup granulated sugar
½ cup molasses
1 tablespoon butter or margarine
1 teaspoon cinnamon
1 teaspoon salt
1 teaspoon nutmeg

About 4 hours before serving: In double-boiler top, scald milk. Slowly stir in cornmeal; cook 20 minutes, stirring occasionally. Preheat oven to 275° F.

To cooked cornmeal, add sugar and remaining ingredients. Pour into greased 1½-quart casserole. Bake, uncovered, for 3 hours, stirring once after 1½ hours. Serve warm or cold with vanilla ice cream, Hard Sauce, page 66, or cream. Makes 6 servings.

❧ INDIAN PUDDING FOR TWO: Preheat oven to 300° F. Halve amounts of ingredients and prepare as above. Bake in greased 1-quart casserole 2½ hours, stirring once after 1½ hours.

❧ GINGER INDIAN PUDDING: Increase sugar to 6 tablespoons; reduce molasses to 6 tablespoons, and substitute 1 teaspoon ginger for cinnamon and nutmeg.

LAZY-DAY APPLE PIE

butter or margarine
1 20-ounce can sliced apples for pie
½ teaspoon cinnamon
⅛ teaspoon salt
⅛ teaspoon nutmeg
2 teaspoons grated lemon peel
1 tablespoon lemon juice
½ teaspoon vanilla extract
granulated sugar
½ 10-ounce package piecrust mix
vanilla ice cream (optional)

is for Pies filled with fruit, cheese or cream

About 2 hours before serving: Preheat oven to 375° F. Lightly butter 9-inch pie plate. In pie plate, toss apples with cinnamon, salt, nutmeg, lemon peel, lemon juice, vanilla and 2 tablespoons of sugar until well mixed. Dot with 1 tablespoon butter.

Sprinkle apple mixture with piecrust mix, then generously sprinkle with sugar. Bake 1 hour.

Serve warm as is, or topped with small scoops of vanilla ice cream. Makes 6 to 8 servings.

FRUITFUL COBBLER

1 quart sliced, peeled peaches,
or sliced, peeled, cored cooking apples,
or sliced, pitted plums
½ teaspoon salt
1 tablespoon all-purpose flour
½ cup corn syrup or honey
1 cup buttermilk-biscuit mix
granulated sugar
½ cup milk or water

About 1½ hours before serving: Preheat oven to 425° F. In 1½-quart casserole, toss peaches with salt, flour and corn syrup. Combine biscuit mix with 2 tablespoons sugar and milk. Pour over peaches; top with 1½ teaspoons sugar. Bake, uncovered, 40 minutes or until topping is golden and fruit tender; serve hot. Makes 8 servings.

◆§ CHERRY: Substitute *two 16-ounce cans drained, pitted sour red cherries* for peaches. Use *honey* instead of corn syrup.

CHOCOLATE DREAM PIE

3 egg whites
¼ teaspoon cream of tartar
dash salt
¾ cup granulated sugar
1 4-ounce package chocolate-flavor
whipped-dessert mix
½ teaspoon orange extract

Day before serving: Preheat oven to 275° F. Beat egg whites until quite stiff; gradually add cream of tartar, salt and sugar, while beating until stiff and satiny.

Spread about two-thirds of this meringue over bottom, up sides of well greased 8-inch pie plate. Drop remaining meringue in mounds on rim of plate, all around, pulling each mound up into points. Bake shell 1 hour or until light brown and crisp. Cool on rack, away from drafts.

Prepare chocolate whipped-dessert mix, as label directs, adding orange extract. Spoon into pie shell; refrigerate. Makes 6 servings.

CRANBERRY STAR CREAM PIE

1 9-inch baked pie shell
1 envelope unflavored gelatin
½ cup granulated sugar
2 egg whites
1 tablespoon lemon juice
⅛ teaspoon salt
1 teaspoon almond extract
1 cup heavy or whipping cream
1 cup cranberry sauce
1½ teaspoons cornstarch

Early in day: Soften gelatin in ¼ cup cold water. In saucepan, boil sugar and ⅓ cup water until mixture forms soft ball when dropped in water (235° F. on candy thermometer); stir in gelatin until dissolved.

In large bowl, with electric mixer at high speed, beat egg whites until stiff peaks form; beat in sugar syrup; beat 1 minute longer. Beat in lemon juice, salt and extract.

In large bowl, with electric mixer at high speed, whip cream until stiff; fold in gelatin mixture. Pour into pie shell; chill until set.

In medium saucepan, heat cranberry sauce and cornstarch, stirring until thickened; cool. Spread over center of pie in shape of star about 4 inches in diameter. Chill. Makes 6 to 8 servings.

ORANGE CONFETTI PIE
pictured between pages 112-113

1 3-ounce package each lemon-flavor
and orange-flavor gelatin
3 cups boiling water
1⅓ cups fine graham-cracker crumbs
¼ cup granulated sugar
¼ cup butter or margarine, softened
1 envelope unflavored gelatin
½ cup fresh orange juice
2 oranges, peeled
1½ cups heavy or whipping cream

Early in day: Prepare lemon and orange gelatins as label directs, but use only 1½ cups boiling water for each package. Pour each gelatin into an 8-inch layer-cake pan; refrigerate until set.

Preheat oven to 375° F. In bowl, mix crumbs and sugar with butter until crumbly; use to line 9-inch pie plate. Bake 8 minutes; cool.

Sprinkle unflavored gelatin over orange juice to soften; stir over hot water until dissolved. Chill until consistency of unbeaten egg white. Section oranges; cut into bite-size pieces; add to gelatin. In bowl, whip 1 cup of the cream until stiff; fold into gelatin mixture.

Cut firm lemon- and orange-gelatin layers into ¾-inch cubes; fold half of cubes into whipped-cream mixture; spoon into pie shell; chill with remaining cubes at least 3 hours, but no longer than 8 hours.

Just before serving: Whip remaining ½ cup cream until stiff; spread over pie; top with remaining gelatin cubes. Makes 6 to 8 servings.

GRAPE CHIFFON PIE

1 9-inch baked pie shell
1 3½-ounce package vanilla-flavor
whipped-dessert mix
¼ cup sweet sherry
1 teaspoon grated lemon peel
1½ cups halved seedless grapes
¾ cup heavy or whipping cream

Early in day: Prepare dessert mix as label directs, substituting ¾ cup cold water and sherry for liquid called for. Fold in grated lemon peel and 1 cup of the grapes. Spoon into pie shell; chill. To serve, whip cream; spread over pie; sprinkle on remaining grapes. Makes one 9-inch pie.

Queen of Puddings, page 115, is a classic English dessert with the taste of strawberries

The refrigerator "bakes" this chocolate-cream-filled Frosted Graham Loaf, page 120

Shimmering cubes of fruit-flavored gelatin in a new guise—Orange Confetti Pie, page 112

Glazed Doughnuts, page 129, light, crisp confections that almost melt in the mouth

For chocolate lovers. Clockwise from top: Chocolate-Filled Cream Puffs, page 28; Walnut-Fudge Wedges, page 134; Chocolate Cup Creams, page 136; Fruited Rounds and Petits Gâteaux, page 135

Three super-delectables: Lemon-Chiffon Chocolate Tarts, page 138; Swedish Double Chocolate Rounds, page 138; Chocolate Fruit Cookies, page 139

A bouquet of Snow Cones, page 140, served with a steaming cup of Cappuccino Napoli, page 26

Truly a work of art, the Vacherin, page 145, a French masterpiece of a meringue

SHIMMERING RUBY PIE

1 9-inch baked pie shell
1 8-ounce package cream cheese, softened
1 tablespoon milk
¼ cup granulated sugar
dash nutmeg
⅛ teaspoon vanilla extract
dash salt
2 medium bananas
1 4¾-ounce package currant-raspberry
Danish dessert
½ cup cranberry-juice cocktail

Early in day: In small bowl, with electric mixer at medium speed, blend together cream cheese, milk, sugar, nutmeg, vanilla and salt. Spread over bottom and up sides of pie shell. Peel and slice bananas; lay them, overlapping, on top of cream-cheese mixture. Make up Danish dessert as label directs, but use 1½ cups water and the cranberry juice as the liquid. Cool slightly; pour over bananas in pie shell. Refrigerate at least 4 hours. Makes 8 servings.

JELLIED FRUIT PIE

1 8-inch baked pie shell, crumb crust,
or Toasted Coconut Crust (below)
1 3-ounce package favorite fruit-flavor
gelatin
2 tablespoons granulated sugar
1 cup boiling water
1½ cups favorite fresh
or canned fruit, drained

Several hours before serving: In medium bowl, dissolve gelatin and sugar in boiling water; stir in 1 cup cold water. Refrigerate, stirring occasionally, until very thick; fold in fruit. (Do not use fresh pineapple.) Pour into cooled pie shell; refrigerate.

To serve: Cut into wedges. Nice with whipped cream. Makes 6 servings.

◄§ TOASTED COCONUT CRUST: *In 8-inch pie plate, spread 2 tablespoons butter or margarine, softened. Into butter, pat 1½ cups flaked coconut to evenly line dish. Bake in 300° F. oven 15 to 20 minutes or until golden. Cool.*

PINK CREAM PIE

1 8-inch baked pie shell
4½ teaspoons unflavored gelatin
granulated sugar
4 eggs, separated
½ cup crème de noyaux liqueur
¼ cup white crème de cacao
red food color
¼ teaspoon salt
1¼ cups heavy or whipping cream

Early in day: In double-boiler top, combine gelatin and ⅓ cup sugar; add slightly beaten egg yolks; mix lightly. Stir in crème de noyaux and crème de cacao. Cook over boiling water, stirring constantly, until mixture thickens, about 5 minutes. Remove from heat and stir for about 10 minutes or until cool. Stir in a few drops of red food color to tint mixture a deep pink.

In large bowl, with rotary beater, beat egg whites until foamy; add salt and beat until soft peaks are formed. Gradually beat in ¼ cup sugar, beating until stiff and glossy.

In bowl, whip 1 cup of the cream until stiff; with rubber spatula or wire whisk, gently fold cream and pink mixture into egg whites. Chill ½ hour, or until mixture mounds when dropped from spoon. Lightly pile gelatin mixture into baked pie shell. Refrigerate.

About ½ hour before serving: Whip remaining ¼ cup cream; use in decorating bag, with decorating tube number 30 in place, to garnish pie. Refrigerate. Makes 8 servings.

BUTTERSCOTCH CREAM PIE

1 9-inch baked pie shell
1 3¾-ounce package butterscotch
pudding-and-pie filling
½ cup coarsely chopped walnuts
1 2-ounce package whipped-topping mix
1 1-ounce square unsweetened chocolate

Early in day: Prepare butterscotch pudding as label directs; cool 5 minutes, stirring occasionally. Stir in walnuts; pour filling into pie shell; refrigerate at least 4 hours or until set.

Just before serving: Prepare whipped topping as label directs; drop by tablespoonfuls, around top of filling, just inside pie edge; sprinkle with chocolate curls made from unsweetened chocolate. Serve, cut in wedges. Makes 6 to 8 servings.

QUEEN OF PUDDINGS
pictured between pages 112-113

2½ cups milk
4 eggs, separated
½ teaspoon vanilla extract
granulated sugar
1 tablespoon grated lemon peel
1 cup fresh white bread crumbs
¼ cup strawberry jam

is for Queen of Puddings, a whole court of others

About 2½ hours before serving: Preheat oven to 325° F. Lightly grease 1½-quart baking dish. In saucepan, warm milk until tiny bubbles form around edges; remove from heat. In bowl, beat yolks, vanilla, ¼ cup sugar and peel; beat in small amount of hot milk. Slowly beat egg mixture back into milk; stir in crumbs; pour into baking dish; place in baking pan with enough boiling water to come to 1 inch from top of dish. Bake 1½ hours or until knife inserted in center comes out clean. Place pudding on rack; cool; spread with jam.

Preheat oven to 350° F. Beat egg whites until soft peaks form; gradually beat in ½ cup sugar, beating until stiff and glossy; cover top of pudding. Bake 10 minutes. Serve warm or cold. Makes 6 servings.

SEMISWEET-COFFEE CUSTARDS

1¼ cups milk
¼ cup granulated sugar
⅛ teaspoon salt
1 6-ounce package semisweet-chocolate pieces
1 egg
1 teaspoon vanilla extract
Coffee Whipped Cream (below)

About 1 hour before serving: In saucepan, combine ¼ cup of the milk with sugar and salt; bring to boiling; remove from heat. Add chocolate pieces; stir until chocolate is melted. With rotary beater, beat in egg and vanilla; gradually stir in remaining 1 cup milk.

Into 4 ungreased 6-ounce custard cups, pour mixture; cover tightly with foil. Set cups in 10-inch or 12-inch skillet in ½-inch hot water. Cover with lid or foil; simmer gently ½ hour. Serve warm right in cups, or chill and then unmold. Top with Coffee Whipped Cream. Makes 4 servings.

❧ COFFEE WHIPPED CREAM: *In small bowl, combine ½ cup heavy or whipping cream, 1 tablespoon confectioners' sugar and ½ teaspoon instant coffee; whip until stiff.*

BRAZILIAN COFFEE CUSTARDS

3 cups milk
1 cup light cream
6 tablespoons instant coffee
2 teaspoons grated orange peel
5 eggs
½ cup granulated sugar
1 teaspoon vanilla extract
1 teaspoon almond extract
½ teaspoon salt
nutmeg
1 cup chopped Brazil nuts
3 tablespoons guava jelly

Early in day: Preheat oven to 325° F. In saucepan, warm milk with cream until tiny bubbles form around edges; add coffee and orange peel; stir well; cool 10 minutes. In bowl, with electric mixer at low speed, slightly beat 4 of the eggs with 1 egg yolk (reserve white for topping) and sugar. Slowly add coffee mixture, then extracts and salt; blend well; strain through fine strainer. Pour into eight 6-ounce custard cups; sprinkle each with nutmeg. Place cups in shallow baking pan on oven rack; fill pan with cold water up to ¾ inch from top of cups. Bake 1 hour or until knife inserted in center comes out clean. Remove from water; cool; refrigerate.

Just before serving: With small spatula, remove each custard from cup and arrange, upside down, on serving dish. Sprinkle with chopped nuts. Beat egg white quite stiff; then beat in jelly until stiff. Swirl over nut-topped custards. Makes 8 servings.

SMALL FRENCH-CHOCOLATE CUSTARDS

4 1-ounce squares unsweetened chocolate
⅔ cup granulated sugar
5 eggs, separated
2 teaspoons rum or cognac

Early in day: In double-boiler top, over hot, *not boiling*, water, melt chocolate; add sugar and ¼ cup water; stir until sugar is dissolved.

In small bowl, with rotary beater, beat egg yolks well. Stirring constantly, slowly pour yolks into chocolate mixture. Remove from heat; stir in rum; cool 5 minutes. Meanwhile, in large bowl, beat egg whites until stiff; fold into cooled chocolate mixture. Pour into 6 custard cups. Refrigerate several hours or overnight. Serve in cups topped with whipped cream, if desired. Makes 6 servings.

CARAMEL-TOPPED CUSTARDS

½ cup granulated sugar
4 eggs
¼ teaspoon salt
1½ cups milk
½ cup light cream
1 teaspoon vanilla extract
chopped walnuts for garnish

About 4 hours before serving: In small skillet over low heat, melt ¼ cup of the sugar, stirring until syrup-like and amber colored. Immediately pour syrup into six lightly greased 5-ounce custard cups.

Preheat oven to 300° F. In bowl, with electric mixer at medium speed, beat eggs until well blended and fluffy; continuing to beat, add salt and remaining ¼ cup sugar; beat until thick and lemon-colored. Stir in milk, cream and vanilla; let stand until any foam settles.

Place cups in baking pan on oven rack; through a fine strainer, pour custard into cups, filling to ½-inch of top. Fill pan with hot water up to ¾ inch from top of cups. Bake 1 hour 10 minutes or until a knife inserted in center of one comes out clean. Cool cups on rack. Refrigerate.

To serve: Run spatula around inside of each custard cup; unmold each custard on dessert plate; garnish with nuts. Makes 6 servings.

MARTHA'S CHERRY BREAD-AND-BUTTER PUDDING

12 slices white bread
butter or margarine, softened
cinnamon
1 10-ounce jar cherry preserves
4 eggs
2⅔ cups milk
2 tablespoons granulated sugar

About 3 hours before serving: Preheat oven to 325° F. Cut crusts from bread; spread each slice, on one side only, with butter. Butter one 8-inch square baking dish. Arrange 4 slices of the bread in bottom of dish; sprinkle them lightly with cinnamon. Spread a spoonful of cherry preserves on each slice. Repeat, making two more layers of 4 buttered slices of bread, cinnamon and preserves.

In bowl, with fork, beat eggs until well blended. Add milk and sugar, stirring until well mixed. Pour egg mixture over bread and bake for 1 hour. Serve warm or cold, with pour cream or whipped cream, if desired. Makes 6 servings.

RICE-PEACH MELBA

⅔ cup packaged precooked rice
2 cups milk
⅓ cup granulated sugar
½ teaspoon salt
⅛ teaspoon nutmeg
⅛ teaspoon cinnamon
½ cup heavy or whipping cream, whipped
1 29-ounce can cling-peach halves, drained
⅓ cup currant jelly, melted

About 45 minutes before serving: In saucepan, combine rice and milk; bring to boiling; cover loosely; boil gently 15 minutes, fluffing rice occasionally with fork.

Remove rice from heat; add sugar, salt, nutmeg and cinnamon. Cool 5 minutes. Spoon into ice-cube tray; chill 20 minutes (be careful not to freeze).

Fold rice mixture into whipped cream. Pile into 6 sherbet glasses; top with peach halves, cut sides down. Pour on melted jelly. Makes 6 servings.

STRAWBERRY CHANTILLY

1 envelope unflavored gelatin
3 tablespoons lemon juice
2 cups milk
¼ cup regular white rice
2 egg yolks, slightly beaten
1 egg white
1 cup heavy or whipping cream, whipped
2 10-ounce packages frozen sliced
strawberries, thawed

Early in day: Soften gelatin in lemon juice; place over hot water and stir until dissolved.

In double-boiler top, in milk, cook rice until tender. Stir small amount of this mixture into egg yolks; return this to rice mixture and cook over hot water, stirring occasionally, until thickened. Stir in gelatin; cool over ice water until mixture mounds.

Beat egg white until stiff. Fold into rice mixture with whipped cream, then fold in strawberries. Refrigerate until serving time. Spoon into serving bowl or sherbet glasses. Makes 6 servings.

STRAWBERRY-CHEESE COUPE

½ cup canned crushed pineapple,
well drained
1 cup cottage cheese
¼ cup granulated sugar
¼ teaspoon almond extract
½ cup heavy or whipping cream, whipped
1 10-ounce package frozen sliced
strawberries, thawed
2 tablespoons grenadine syrup

is for

Refrigerator desserts, all

ready to serve

Several hours before serving: In medium bowl, combine pineapple, cheese, sugar and almond extract. Fold in whipped cream. Refrigerate.
In small bowl, combine strawberries and grenadine. Refrigerate.
At serving time: In sherbet or parfait glasses, alternate layers of cottage-cheese mixture and strawberries. If desired, top each serving with a strawberry. Makes 6 servings.

MACAROON RUSSE

14 ladyfingers, split
⅓ cup sherry
½ cup butter or margarine, softened
1 cup confectioners' sugar
2 egg yolks, unbeaten
1 whole egg
½ cup chopped toasted almonds
2 cups macaroon crumbs
2 egg whites
1 cup heavy or whipping cream, whipped

Day before: Line bottom and sides of 2-quart bowl or mold with half of split ladyfingers; sprinkle with 2 tablespoons of the sherry.
In large bowl, with electric mixer at medium speed, beat butter with sugar until light and fluffy. Beat in egg yolks, one at a time, then whole egg; add almonds, crumbs and remaining sherry.
In small bowl, beat egg whites until stiff; fold into creamed mixture, then fold in whipped cream.
Turn half of this mixture into prepared bowl; top with rest of split ladyfingers, then rest of mixture. Refrigerate.
To serve: Unmold onto serving plate. Garnish, if desired, with additional whipped cream and slivered almonds. Makes 8 to 10 servings.

FROSTED GRAHAM LOAF
pictured between pages 112-113

1½ pints heavy or whipping cream
6 tablespoons cocoa
dash salt
8 tablespoons granulated sugar
50 graham-cracker squares
2 1-ounce squares semisweet chocolate

Day before: In chilled bowl, with electric mixer or rotary beater, beat cream with cocoa, salt and sugar until thick and of spreading consistency. Refrigerate one third of this frosting mixture.

With remaining frosting, spread one side of 25 of the graham crackers with a layer about ¼-inch thick. On platter, put crackers together, sandwich fashion with frosting between, on edge in one continuous row. Spread some frosting along inside of row. Frost remaining 25 crackers and put them together in the same way, placing this row up against the frosting on the first row, in a parallel line.

With refrigerated third of frosting, cover sides and top of loaf; top with chocolate curls prepared from semisweet chocolate. Refrigerate.

To serve: Cut loaf at an angle into ½- to ¾-inch-thick slices. If desired, slices can be cut in half in center. Makes 12 servings.

PICCADILLY TRIFLE

1 29-ounce can pear halves
1 3¼-ounce package vanilla
pudding-and-pie filling
3 cups milk
sherry
⅔ cup seedless black raspberry jam
2 6-inch spongecake layers
⅔ cup heavy or whipping cream, whipped
candied cherries for garnish

Early in day: Drain pears, reserving ½ cup of the syrup. Reserve.

Prepare pudding as label directs, but use 3 cups milk; cool; stir in sherry to taste. In serving bowl, place one of the cake layers; spread with half the jam; sprinkle with half the pear syrup; top with half the pears; pour half the pudding over all. Repeat layers. Refrigerate.

To serve: Top with whipped cream; garnish with sliced cherries. Serve in wedges with some of the sauce left in bowl. Makes 9 servings.

WHITE MOUNTAIN PUDDING

2 quarts milk
1 cup uncooked farina
1¼ cups granulated sugar
salt
½ teaspoon almond extract
2 teaspoons nutmeg
1 30-ounce can purple plums
¼ cup cornstarch
1 cup light corn syrup
2 teaspoons almond extract
red food color
seedless grapes for garnish

Day before: In large saucepan, bring milk to boiling. Gradually add farina, stirring constantly. Stir in 1 cup of the granulated sugar, 1½ teaspoons salt and almond extract; sprinkle in nutmeg. Cook over low heat, stirring constantly, 10 minutes or until very thick. Pour mixture into greased, 2-quart mold; cool; refrigerate.

About ½ hour before serving: Drain plum juice into 2-cup measure; add water to make 2 cups, if needed. In saucepan, combine remaining ¼ cup granulated sugar, cornstarch and ¼ teaspoon salt. Gradually stir in plum-juice mixture, corn syrup and extract. Cook over low heat, stirring constantly, until clear and thickened. Stir in few drops of food color.

Set pudding mold in hot water for 2 minutes; unmold on serving platter. Garnish with drained plums and tiny bunches of grapes. Spoon some sauce over pudding; pass rest. Makes 10 to 12 servings.

OLD-FASHIONED BLANCMANGE

2 cups milk
2 tablespoons cocoa
¼ cup granulated sugar
¼ teaspoon salt
1½ tablespoons cornstarch
1 egg
⅛ teaspoon almond extract
½ teaspoon vanilla extract
½ cup heavy or whipping cream

Early in day: In double-boiler top, over direct heat, scald 1¾ cups of the milk. Combine cocoa, 2 tablespoons of the sugar, salt and cornstarch; gradually add remaining ¼ cup milk, stirring until smooth; stir into scalded milk. Cook, stirring constantly, until thickened.

In small bowl, beat egg with remaining 2 tablespoons sugar until well blended; stirring constantly, slowly add to chocolate mixture. Cook over boiling water, stirring, until smooth and thickened, about 2 minutes; cool. Stir in extracts; whip ¼ cup of cream; fold in. Spoon into serving dish or sherbet glasses; chill.

To serve: Whip remaining ¼ cup cream. Top pudding with swirl of whipped cream. Makes 4 to 6 servings.

RASPBERRY-RIBBONED CRÈME

1 8-ounce package cream cheese, softened
½ cup granulated sugar
1 envelope unflavored gelatin
1 cup milk
4 teaspoons lemon juice
1 teaspoon vanilla extract
1 cup heavy or whipping cream
1 cup bottled raspberry fruit syrup
3 tablespoons cornstarch
red food color

Day before: Heavily grease 5-cup fluted oval mold; set aside. With electric mixer at medium speed, beat cream cheese with sugar until fluffy. Meanwhile, soften gelatin in ⅓ cup water; stirring constantly, dissolve gelatin over hot water; remove from heat; set aside.

With electric mixer at low speed, gradually beat milk, 3 teaspoons of the lemon juice and vanilla into cheese mixture; beat in dissolved gelatin.

Whip cream until soft peaks form; fold into gelatin mixture, then turn into mold; refrigerate.

About 1 hour before serving: In saucepan, heat fruit syrup and ½ cup water. Dissolve cornstarch in 3 tablespoons cold water; stir into hot mixture; bring to boiling, stirring constantly, until slightly thickened and clear; stir in remaining teaspoon of lemon juice and enough food color to make bright red. Cover with waxed paper; cool at room temperature.

To serve: Run a wet pointed knife between gelatin and mold to loosen; with wet fingers, gently pull gelatin away from mold all the way around. Dip mold in and out of warm water; unmold on serving plate.

Drizzle sauce over mold (add a little water if sauce is too thick). Cut mold in wedges; pass remaining sauce. Makes 10 servings.

JELLIED FRUIT MOLD

1 29-ounce can pear halves
port wine
1 3-ounce package each lemon-flavor
and cherry-flavor gelatin
1 10-ounce package frozen raspberries
1 banana, peeled and sliced

Day before or early in day: Drain pear syrup into 2-cup measure; add enough wine to syrup to make 2 cups. In saucepan, bring 1 cup of this liquid to boiling; remove from heat; add lemon gelatin, stir until it dissolves. Add remaining cup of liquid. In 3-quart mold, with cut sides up, arrange pears; cover with half of lemon-gelatin mixture. Refrigerate remaining gelatin and mold until gelatin in mold is almost set. Pour on remaining lemon gelatin. Refrigerate until almost set.

Meanwhile, in bowl, dissolve cherry gelatin in 1 cup hot water; add ½ cup cold water, frozen raspberries and banana. Refrigerate, stirring occasionally, until thick and syrupy, then pour over almost-set pear layer. Refrigerate until firm.

To serve: Unmold on serving platter. Makes 8 servings.

FRUITED CRÈME BRÛLÉE

3 cups heavy or whipping cream
6 egg yolks
6 tablespoons granulated sugar
1 teaspoon vanilla extract
½ cup packed light brown sugar
choice of fruits

Early in day: In bottom of large double boiler, scald cream. In double-boiler top, with rotary beater, beat egg yolks and sugar until blended; slowly stir in scalded cream. Cook over hot, *not boiling*, water, stirring constantly, until thick as heavy cream. Add vanilla; mix well. Pour into shallow 1½-quart glass baking dish; refrigerate.

Several hours before serving: Preheat broiler, if manufacturer directs, with rack removed. Carefully sift brown sugar over custard; place dish on broiler rack; return to broiling pan; broil 4 minutes or until sugar melts, making a shiny caramel glaze on top. Chill.

To serve: Place cold custard or "brûlée" in center of tray; surround it with one or more fruits: sweetened fresh strawberries, pineapple chunks, raspberries, peach halves, pears or orange chunks. Serve brûlée spooned over individual servings of fruit. Makes 6 servings.

CUSTARD SAUCE

2 cups milk or 1 cup undiluted evaporated milk
plus 1 cup water
3 eggs or 6 egg yolks
about ¼ cup granulated sugar
¼ teaspoon salt
1 teaspoon vanilla extract
or ½ teaspoon almond extract

is for Sauces
to top your creations

Early in day: In double-boiler top over direct heat, warm milk until tiny bubbles form around edges.

In medium bowl, with fork, beat eggs slightly; stir in sugar (amount depends on taste) and salt. Slowly add hot milk, stirring constantly to prevent cooked-egg specks;* pour back into double-boiler top. Cook over hot, *not boiling*, water, stirring constantly, until mixture coats spoon. Pour into chilled bowl; cool; add vanilla; cover; refrigerate.

To serve: Spoon over pudding, cut-up fruit, cake, gelatin, etc. Makes 2 cups sauce or sixteen 2-tablespoon servings.

*If finished custard is lumpy or curdles, strain through fine sieve into bowl or pan; place over cold water and beat with a rotary beater until smooth (custard may be a little thinner than it was).

✑ CUSTARD SAUCE DELUXE: Prepare sauce as above, but substitute *1 cup heavy or whipping cream, 1 cup milk, 4 egg yolks, ¼ cup granulated sugar, 1 tablespoon flour, ¼ teaspoon salt* for ingredients above. Flavor with *3 tablespoons sherry.*

LEMON SAUCE

½ cup granulated sugar
¼ teaspoon salt
3 tablespoons cornstarch
2 cups boiling water
¼ cup butter or margarine
1 tablespoon grated lemon peel
3 tablespoons lemon juice
dash nutmeg (optional)

About 1 hour before serving: In medium saucepan, combine sugar, salt and cornstarch. Stirring constantly, slowly add boiling water until mixture is smooth and well blended. Simmer over medium heat, stirring constantly, for 5 minutes or until clear and thickened; remove from heat. Stir in butter, lemon peel and juice and nutmeg, if desired. Serve warm, or refrigerate. Makes about 2 cups.

VANILLA SAUCE

½ cup granulated sugar
¼ teaspoon salt
2 tablespoons cornstarch
2 cups boiling water
¼ cup butter or margarine
dash nutmeg or mace
2 teaspoons vanilla extract

About 15 minutes before serving: In saucepan, combine sugar, salt and cornstarch; gradually stir in water; bring to boiling, stirring constantly, about 5 minutes, until smooth and thickened. Stir in butter and remaining ingredients. Serve hot, spooned over spice cake, steamed pudding, fruit desserts, etc. Makes about 2½ cups.

◦§ HOLIDAY: Omit vanilla and nutmeg or mace. Add *rum, sherry or brandy* to taste.

◦§ ORANGE: *In saucepan, combine ½ cup granulated sugar, dash each salt and cinnamon and 1 tablespoon cornstarch. Stir in ¾ cup boiling water; proceed as above; when thickened, add 2 tablespoons butter, 1 teaspoon grated orange peel, ¼ cup orange juice and 1 tablespoon lemon juice. Makes about 1 cup.*

BING-CHERRY SAUCE

About 20 minutes before serving: In skillet, melt ¾ cup *currant jelly;* add one 29-ounce can pitted *Bing cherries,* drained. Stirring, slowly bring to boiling. Serve warm on ice cream, custards, etc. Makes 3½ cups.

ICE-CREAM SAUCE

1 egg
¼ cup granulated sugar
dash salt
⅓ cup melted butter or margarine
1 teaspoon vanilla or
brandy extract
1 cup heavy or whipping cream, whipped

Just before serving: Beat egg until thick and light; beat in sugar and salt. Gradually beat in butter, extract. Fold in cream. Serve on warm chocolate or white-cake squares. Makes about 2 cups.

MELBA SAUCE

1 10-ounce package frozen raspberries, thawed
½ cup currant jelly
1½ teaspoons cornstarch

Early in day: In saucepan, crush raspberries. Add jelly; over low heat, bring to boiling. Blend cornstarch with 1 tablespoon water; add to berry mixture. Cook, stirring constantly, until clear and thickened. Strain if desired; cool, then refrigerate. Serve on lemon sherbet, rice pudding or custard. Makes about 2 cups.

RUM SAUCE

¾ cup heavy or whipping cream
1½ teaspoons all-purpose flour
⅛ teaspoon salt
3 tablespoons granulated sugar
3 egg yolks, lightly beaten
3 tablespoons rum

Early in day: In double-boiler top over direct heat, warm cream until tiny bubbles form around edges. In bowl, mix flour, salt and sugar. Stirring constantly, gradually add yolks, then hot cream. Return all to double-boiler top. Continuing to stir, cook over hot, *not boiling*, water until mixture thickens slightly and coats a spoon. Pour at once into small bowl; cover with waxed paper placed directly on surface of sauce. Refrigerate until serving time, then stir in rum. Delicious over Coffee Jelly (page 43) , steamed pudding, etc. Makes about 1 cup.

EASY CHOCOLATE SAUCE

1 6-ounce package semisweet-chocolate
pieces (1 cup)
½ to ¾ cup light corn syrup
¼ cup light cream
1 tablespoon butter or margarine
¼ teaspoon vanilla extract

About 20 minutes before serving: In double-boiler top, over hot, *not boiling*, water, melt chocolate with corn syrup, stirring until smooth and well blended. Stir in cream, butter and vanilla. Serve warm over chocolate, coffee or peppermint ice cream. Makes about 1½ cups.

BUTTER CREAM SAUCE

1 cup granulated sugar
½ cup butter or margarine
½ cup light cream
1 teaspoon vanilla extract

About 15 minutes before serving: In saucepan, combine sugar, butter, cream and vanilla. Bring to boiling. Serve hot, on puddings, gingerbread, etc. Makes about 1½ cups.

⋘ QUICK RUM: Just before serving, stir in *2 to 3 tablespoons rum* and a *dash of nutmeg.*

SUNSHINE FOAMY SAUCE

1 egg, separated
dash salt
¼ cup packed brown sugar
¼ cup heavy or whipping cream, whipped
½ teaspoon vanilla extract

About 15 minutes before serving: In medium bowl, with rotary beater, beat egg white with salt until foamy; slowly add 2 tablespoons of the sugar, beating until sugar is dissolved and stiff peaks form.

In small bowl, with same beater, beat egg yolk with remaining 2 tablespoons sugar until light; fold into egg-white mixture, then fold in the whipped cream and vanilla. Serve over steamed pudding, warm gingerbread, chocolate cake, etc. Makes about 1 cup.

QUICK BUTTERSCOTCH SAUCE

¼ cup evaporated milk, undiluted
¼ cup light corn syrup
1 6-ounce package butterscotch pieces (1 cup)
2 tablespoons slivered,
crystallized ginger (optional)

About 20 minutes before serving: In saucepan over medium heat, bring evaporated milk and corn syrup to boiling, stirring. Remove from heat; add butterscotch pieces; stir until melted. Add ginger. Serve warm or cold over ice cream, angel-cake squares, etc. Makes about 1 cup.

HOT FUDGE SAUCE

2 1-ounce squares unsweetened chocolate
1½ cups corn syrup
⅛ teaspoon salt
1 teaspoon vanilla extract

About ½ hour before serving: In saucepan over low heat, melt chocolate in ½ cup water, stirring constantly until smooth and thickened,
about 2 minutes. Remove from heat; gradually blend in syrup and salt.
Simmer 10 minutes, stirring often. Add vanilla. Serve hot or cold, on
ice cream, cream puffs, warm cake squares, etc. Makes about 1½ cups.

BUTTER-CARAMEL SAUCE

¾ cup granulated sugar
¼ cup butter or margarine
⅛ teaspoon salt
½ cup light corn syrup
1 cup light cream
½ teaspoon vanilla extract

About ½ hour before serving: In small saucepan, combine sugar, butter,
salt, syrup and ½ cup of the cream. Cook over low heat, stirring fre-
quently, until a little of the mixture forms a hard ball in cold water, or
to 250° F. on candy thermometer. Add remaining ½ cup cream; cook
until a little of the mixture forms a thread when dropped from spoon,
or to 216° F. on candy thermometer. Remove from heat. Add vanilla.

Serve warm on ice cream, baked custard, warm cake squares, cream
puffs, etc. Makes about 2 cups.

SIMPLE HARD SAUCE

⅓ cup butter or margarine
1 cup confectioners' sugar
½ teaspoon vanilla extract or lemon extract

Several hours before serving: In small bowl, with spoon or electric mixer,
beat butter with sugar until light and creamy; beat in extract. Spoon into
serving dish. Refrigerate until firm.

To serve: If desired, shape into small balls and roll in grated orange
peel, or pass in serving dish with spoon. Serve on fruit cobblers, steamed
pudding, bread pudding, etc. Makes about ¾ cup.

GLAZED DOUGHNUTS
pictured between pages 112-113

4 cups all-purpose flour,
sifted before measuring
¼ cup granulated sugar
1 teaspoon salt
1 package active dry yeast
¾ cup milk
¼ cup butter or margarine
2 eggs
1 teaspoon grated lemon peel
salad oil for deep frying
1 cup sifted confectioners' sugar
½ teaspoon vanilla extract

is for Tidbits
too good to resist

Early in day: In large bowl, combine 1 cup of the flour, granulated sugar, salt and yeast. In saucepan over low heat, heat ¼ cup water with milk and butter until butter melts and liquid is very warm (120° to 130° F.). With electric mixer at medium speed, gradually add liquid to dry ingredients. Beat 2 minutes, scraping bowl occasionally. Add eggs, one at a time, beating after each addition. Gradually beat in 1½ cups of the flour. Beat 2 minutes at high speed, scraping bowl.

With spoon, stir in lemon peel and 1¼ cups of the flour. Turn out onto lightly floured surface; knead a few times. If dough seems sticky, work in remaining ¼ cup flour. Shape dough into ball; place in large greased bowl; turn to grease top of dough. Cover with towel; let rise in warm place (80° to 85° F.) away from draft, until doubled, about 1½ hours. (Dough has risen enough when two fingers pressed lightly into center of dough leave a hole.) Meanwhile, cut sixteen 3½-inch squares of waxed paper.

Turn out dough onto lightly floured surface. Divide dough in fourths; refrigerate three-fourths. With hands, roll out remaining fourth into a single strand; cut into 8 equal pieces; with hands, roll each piece into a strand 8 inches long. Twist every two strands together, forming a twisted circle, as pictured; turn ends under. Place each circle on a waxed-paper square on cookie sheet. Repeat with remaining dough. Cover with clean towel. Let rise until doubled.

Into Dutch oven, pour 1½ inches of salad oil; heat to 350° F. on deep-fat thermometer, or until a cube of day-old bread browns in 60 seconds. Hold circle of dough close to surface of oil; slip circle from paper into oil. Fry 3 doughnuts at a time, enlarging center holes if necessary. When brown, turn and brown other side; drain on paper towels.

In bowl, combine confectioners' sugar and vanilla with 1½ tablespoons water; beat until smooth. With pastry brush, brush on warm doughnuts. Or sprinkle doughnuts with granulated sugar. Makes 16 doughnuts.

BEIGNETS

½ cup butter or margarine
¼ teaspoon salt
1 teaspoon granulated sugar
1 cup plus 2 tablespoons all-purpose flour,
sifted before measuring
1 teaspoon vanilla extract
4 eggs
salad oil for deep frying
confectioners' sugar

About 20 minutes before serving: In saucepan, bring butter, salt, sugar and 1 cup water to boiling. Remove pan from heat; add flour all at once, stirring vigorously until ingredients are combined thoroughly and dough leaves sides of pan and forms ball. Add vanilla, then eggs, one at a time, stirring vigorously. Dough should be smooth and glossy.

Meanwhile, in deep skillet, heat about 1½ inches salad oil to 375° F. on deep-fat thermometer, or heat oil in electric skillet. Drop heaping teaspoonfuls of dough into hot oil and fry beignets, a few at a time, until golden. (Beignets will puff up to about 2 inches in diameter when done.) Drain on paper towels.

Dust beignets with confectioners' sugar. Arrange in serving bowl and serve warm. Makes 10 to 12 servings.

CHOCOLATE-COCONUT BUTTERBALLS

1 cup butter or margarine, softened
6 tablespoons confectioners' sugar
2 cups all-purpose flour
1 teaspoon vanilla extract
1 4-ounce package sweet cooking chocolate,
coarsely chopped
1 cup toasted sweetened coconut

Early in day: Preheat oven to 350° F. In large bowl, with electric mixer at medium speed, beat butter with ¼ cup of the sugar until creamy and smooth. Reduce speed to low; beat in flour and vanilla until well blended; beat in chocolate and ⅔ cup of the coconut.

Shape the mixture into small balls, about ¾ inch in diameter. Place on ungreased cookie sheets, about 1 inch apart; bake 15 minutes, or until lightly browned. Sprinkle cookies with remaining sugar and coconut. Makes about 6 dozen cookies.

MINCEMEAT-TOPPED SHORTBREAD

¾ cup butter or margarine, softened
¼ cup granulated sugar
2 cups all-purpose flour,
sifted before measuring
1⅓ cups prepared mincemeat
2 tablespoons brandy

Early in day: In bowl, beat butter and sugar until light. With pastry blender, cut in flour. Shape into flat circle; chill ½ hour.

Preheat oven to 350° F. On lightly floured surface, roll dough into circle ¼ inch thick; place on ungreased cookie sheet; cut into 8 pie-shape wedges. To decorate top, lightly press a fancy cookie cutter repeatedly into surface. Bake 25 minutes; cool on rack. Arrange wedges on cake plate; cover with waxed paper and store at room temperature.

About 10 minutes before serving: In small saucepan, warm mincemeat; stir in brandy. Serve spooned over wedges. Makes 8 servings.

FASTNACHTCHÜECHLI (Large Fried Cookie)

6 eggs
6 tablespoons heavy or whipping cream
½ teaspoon salt
3¾ cups all-purpose flour,
sifted before measuring
salad oil for deep frying
confectioners' sugar

Day before serving: In large bowl, with electric mixer or rotary beater, beat eggs until thick and lemon-colored. Add cream and salt, then 3 cups of the flour; with spoon, beat until smooth. With hands, slowly knead in remaining ¾ cup flour, mixing well. Cover; refrigerate.

Early in day: Cut dough into walnut-size balls; let come to room temperature. On floured 9-inch square of waxed paper, with stockinette-covered rolling pin, roll one ball of the dough into as thin a circle as possible (about 8 inches in diameter); chill right on the paper. Repeat with remaining balls of dough.

When dough is thoroughly chilled, in large skillet, heat 1 inch of oil to 370° F. on deep-fat thermometer, or until a cube of day-old bread browns in about 45 seconds. Remove circle of dough from refrigerator; peel off paper. To get edges as thin as possible, with hands, gently stretch dough into a slightly larger circle. Drop into hot oil and fry until golden on each side. While still warm, sprinkle one side with sugar. Repeat with other circles of dough. Makes about 20 cookies.

ROSETTES
pictured between pages 48-49

salad oil for deep frying
1 cup milk
2 eggs
1 tablespoon vanilla extract
1 cup all-purpose flour
2 teaspoons granulated sugar
¼ teaspoon salt
confectioners' sugar

About 20 minutes before serving: In electric Dutch oven, deep electric skillet or large saucepan, heat about 2 inches of salad oil to 400° F.

In electric-blender container (or small bowl), put milk and next 5 ingredients. Cover; blend (or beat) until smooth; pour into pie plate.

In hot oil, heat rosette iron 2 minutes; dip into batter to about ¾ of rosette form, then quickly plunge into hot oil, being careful not to touch bottom of pan. When active bubbling stops, remove iron from pan. With fork, gently ease rosette from iron; drain on paper towels. Repeat until all the batter is used. Dust with confectioners' sugar. Makes about 70 rosettes.

STRUFOLI or PIGNOLATA

4 to 5 cups all-purpose flour
2 teaspoons double-acting baking powder
1 teaspoon salt
3 tablespoons white wine
1 quart salad oil
6 eggs, beaten
1 24-ounce jar honey
½ cup pine nuts
colored sprinkles
candied cherries

Several days before serving: Onto pastry board, sift 4 cups of the flour with baking powder and salt. Make well in center; pour in wine and ¼ cup of the salad oil; gradually add eggs, blending them with a fork into the flour along with the wine and oil. Knead until soft and smooth and well blended. Divide dough in half; cover one half with a damp cloth. On well-floured surface, roll other half to ¼ inch thickness; cut into strips ½-inch wide. With palms of hands, roll each strip into pencil-shaped roll. With floured knife, cut each roll into ¼-inch pieces.

In deep saucepan, heat rest of salad oil to 350° F. on deep-fat thermometer, or until a cube of day-old bread browns in 60 seconds. Drop in pieces of dough, stirring to brown evenly. Remove with slotted spoon; drain on paper towels. Repeat with remaining half of dough. Place all fried balls or Strufoli in large bowl.

In saucepan, simmer honey to 250° F. on a candy thermometer, or until a little of the mixture, dropped in cold water, forms a soft ball. Remove from heat; add pine nuts; pour over Strufoli, tossing to coat well.

Let stand, covered, for 12 to 24 hours or up to a week or so.

At serving time, heap them in a large serving dish or individual paper cups. Top with colored sprinkles and candied cherries. Serve with paper napkins close by. They are irresistible nibblers for dessert time. Makes about 13 cups.

To Vary: You may omit *¼ cup salad oil in making dough. Or add 1 cup chopped walnuts and/or some semisweet-chocolate pieces to the* heated honey before pouring it over the Strufoli.

GERMAN BAR COOKIES

4 cups all-purpose flour
2½ teaspoons double-acting baking powder
1 cup granulated sugar
1 cup salad oil
4 eggs
1 tablespoon grated orange peel
1 teaspoon vanilla extract
¼ teaspoon salt
2 tablespoons chocolate syrup

Day before serving: Sift together flour and baking powder. In large bowl, with electric mixer at medium speed, combine sugar, oil, eggs, orange peel, vanilla and salt; beat in 2 cups flour mixture; with wooden spoon, stir in remaining flour. Measure ½ cup dough into small bowl; stir in chocolate syrup until well mixed. Cover; refrigerate both doughs several hours or overnight.

Several hours before serving: Preheat oven to 350° F. On floured, large cookie sheet, pat plain dough into three 8″ by 4″ rectangles. With fingers, pull one-third chocolate dough into little pieces and place at one end of each rectangle. Starting at chocolate end, roll up dough, jelly-roll fashion; flatten slightly.

Bake 20 minutes. Remove from oven; immediately cut each on a slant crosswise into ½-inch bars. Return to oven and bake 15 minutes or until golden. Remove to rack to cool. Makes 30 cookies.

WALNUT-FUDGE WEDGES
pictured between pages 112-113

1 cup sweet butter, softened
1½ cups sifted confectioners' sugar
8 eggs, separated
6 1-ounce squares semisweet chocolate, melted
2 cups walnuts, finely chopped
3 tablespoons all-purpose flour
1½ teaspoons vanilla extract
Chocolate-Walnut Filling (below)
Thin Chocolate Glaze (below)
16 walnut halves

Day before or early in day: Preheat oven to 325° F. Grease and flour three 9-inch layer cake pans. In large bowl, with electric mixer at medium speed, beat butter until creamy; gradually add sugar, beating well after each addition. In small bowl, with electric mixer at high speed, beat egg yolks until light and lemon-colored. Beat into butter-sugar mixture along with melted chocolate, chopped walnuts, flour and vanilla.

In medium bowl, with electric mixer at high speed, beat egg whites until soft peaks form; fold them, about one-fourth at a time, into the egg-butter-sugar mixture above. Divide batter evenly among prepared pans. Bake 35 minutes, or until cake tester inserted in center comes out clean. Cool on racks 10 minutes; remove from pans; finish cooling.

Meanwhile, make filling. Brush cake layers free of crumbs; spread cooled filling over 2 of the layers; stack, then top with third layer. Make chocolate glaze; quickly spread while warm over top and down sides of cake. Garnish with walnut halves. Refrigerate.

To serve: Cut into thin wedges. Makes 16 servings.

CHOCOLATE-WALNUT FILLING

In double-boiler top, over hot, *not boiling,* water, melt *two 1-ounce squares semisweet chocolate.* Stir in *⅓ cup granulated sugar, 2 cups finely chopped walnuts* and *½ cup milk.* Cook over boiling water, 5 minutes, or until sugar is dissolved. Remove from heat; beat in *¼ cup butter or margarine, softened,* and *1 teaspoon vanilla extract.* Cool.

THIN CHOCOLATE GLAZE

In double-boiler top, over hot, *not boiling,* water, melt *one 6-ounce package semisweet-chocolate pieces* with *2 tablespoons butter or margarine;* remove from heat; beat in *2 tablespoons light corn syrup* and *3 tablespoons milk* until smooth and well blended.

FRUITED ROUNDS
pictured between pages 112-113

1 18.5-ounce package
dark chocolate-fudge cake mix
⅓ cup apple jelly, melted
6 canned pear halves or 1 11-ounce can
mandarin-orange sections
whipped topping

Early in day: Preheat oven as cake-mix label directs. Grease, then flour
15½" by 10½" jelly-roll pan. Prepare cake mix as label directs; bake in
jelly-roll pan 25 to 30 minutes, or until cake tester inserted in center
comes out clean. Cool in pan 10 minutes; with knife, loosen sides; invert
on board to cool completely.

With 2¾-inch round cookie cutter, cut out 6 rounds, crosswise of
cake, in two rows; wrap well; refrigerate. (Use remaining cake to prepare Petits Gâteaux, below.)

To serve: Brush chocolate rounds with some melted jelly. Top each
with a well-drained pear half, cut side down, or 6 to 8 well-drained
mandarin-orange sections, as pictured. Brush fruit with jelly. If desired,
garnish each Fruited Round with whipped topping. Makes 6 servings.

PETITS GÂTEAUX
pictured between pages 112-113

chocolate cake left from Fruited Rounds (above)
2 2-ounce packages whipped-topping mix
½ cup undiluted evaporated milk
dash salt
1 6-ounce package semisweet-chocolate
pieces (1 cup)
1 teaspoon vanilla extract

Up to 4 hours before serving: Trim edges from chocolate cake to make
a rectangle. Prepare topping mix, one package at a time, as label directs;
spread evenly, only on top of cake. Chill for at least one hour.

In small saucepan, bring milk and salt to boiling. Remove from heat;
stir in chocolate pieces until mixture is smooth and well blended; add
vanilla. Cool this glaze about 5 minutes, or until lukewarm.

With broad spatula, spread enough glaze over whipped topping to
coat top only; refrigerate cake. (Leftover glaze can be reheated over hot
water, then drizzled over ice cream or spread on cookies.)

Serve cake cut into 9 to 12 rectangles. Makes 9 to 12 servings.

CHOCOLATE-CUP CREAMS
pictured between pages 112-113

8 packaged fluted 3-inch paper baking cups
1 6-ounce package semisweet-chocolate
pieces (1 cup)
1 tablespoon shortening
1 envelope unflavored gelatin
1 3¼-ounce package vanilla
pudding-and-pie filling
2 cups light cream
1 teaspoon instant-coffee powder
1 cup heavy or whipping cream
chocolate shot
8 maraschino cherries with stems

Several days before serving: Set one paper cup in each 3″ by 1¼″ muffin-pan cup. In double-boiler top, over hot, *not boiling*, water, melt chocolate pieces with shortening; keep warm. Starting from top rim of each paper cup, drizzle chocolate, 1 heaping measuring teaspoonful at a time, down inside of cup; about 3 of these heaping teaspoons will cover entire inside of each cup. Refrigerate.

Early in day: Remove paper cups, one at a time, from muffin pan; gently, but quickly, peel away paper, leaving a chocolate cup. Set cups on a platter; refrigerate.

Sprinkle gelatin in 2 tablespoons cold water to soften. In saucepan, prepare pudding as label directs, but substitute the light cream above for the milk called for on label. Stir in softened gelatin and instant-coffee powder until both are completely dissolved. Lay a piece of waxed paper directly on surface of pudding; refrigerate until *just cool*. Whip cream; fold into pudding.

Fill each chocolate cup with about ¼ cup of pudding mixture. (Spoon rest into custard cups to serve another day.) Refrigerate all.

Just before serving: Garnish each chocolate cup with a few chocolate shot, then a cherry. Makes 8 servings.

FRUITCAKE MINIATURES

Early in day: Cut ½ pound dark fruitcake into 1-inch cubes. In small bowl, thoroughly mix ¾ cup sifted confectioners' sugar, ½ teaspoon cocoa, ½ teaspoon vanilla extract and 3 to 4 teaspoons water until smooth and frosting-like. Dribble 1 heaping teaspoonful of frosting mixture over each cube, covering top and sides; top with a *cashew* (you'll need about ½ pound). Let stand one hour to set. Store, tightly covered. Makes about 20 cubes.

NUTTY SQUARES

½ cup all-purpose flour
½ teaspoon double-acting baking powder
½ teaspoon salt
2 eggs
½ cup granulated sugar
½ teaspoon vanilla extract
1 12-ounce package
dried, pitted prunes, cut up
1 cup coarsely chopped walnuts
confectioners' sugar

Early in day: Preheat oven to 325° F. Grease an 8-inch square baking pan. Sift flour with baking powder and salt.

In bowl, with electric mixer at medium speed, beat eggs until foamy; gradually add sugar, beating constantly. Add flour mixture; mix well. Stir in vanilla, prunes and walnuts. Spread in baking pan. Bake 40 minutes. While warm, cut into squares and sprinkle with confectioners' sugar. Makes 16.

JELLY TARTS

2½ cups all-purpose flour,
sifted before measuring
½ teaspoon salt
¼ teaspoon double-acting baking powder
1 cup shortening
2 teaspoons vanilla extract
½ cup sifted confectioners' sugar
milk
currant or mint jelly

Early in day: Sift flour with salt and baking powder. With electric mixer at medium speed, beat shortening with vanilla and sugar until creamy. Beat in flour mixture and ¼ cup milk. Shape into 2 balls; wrap in foil; refrigerate until easy to handle, about 2 hours.

Preheat oven to 350° F. On lightly floured surface, let dough stand at room temperature 5 minutes; with floured, stockinette-covered rolling pin, roll to ¼-inch thickness. Cut into 2½-inch rounds. From center of half of the rounds, cut ¾-inch round; brush rings with milk. Reroll centers with leftover trimmings from dough as above.

Place rings and 2½-inch rounds on ungreased cookie sheet, 1 inch apart. Bake 15 to 18 minutes; cool. Place 1 teaspoonful of jelly in center of rounds; top each with ring. Makes about 1 dozen.

SWEDISH DOUBLE-CHOCOLATE ROUNDS
pictured between pages 112-113

1½ cups butter or margarine
granulated sugar
2 eggs
⅔ cup blanched almonds, ground
½ teaspoon almond extract
5 cups all-purpose flour,
sifted before measuring
1 4-ounce bar sweet cooking chocolate
⅓ cup slivered toasted almonds
1 envelope unflavored gelatin
1½ tablespoons cocoa
1 cup heavy or whipping cream
½ teaspoon vanilla extract
2 egg whites

Day before: Preheat oven to 375° F. In large bowl, with electric mixer at low speed, cream butter with 1½ cups sugar until light and fluffy. Beat in eggs, ground almonds and almond extract; add flour, mixing well.

On floured surface, roll half of dough (use rest in Lemon Chiffon Tarts below) into round ¼-inch thick. With 2¾-inch round cookie cutter, cut out 30 cookies. Bake on ungreased cookie sheets about 12 minutes, or until lightly browned. Cool on racks. Store, uncovered.

Early in day: In small, heavy saucepan over low heat, stirring constantly, melt chocolate in 2 tablespoons water; use to frost cookies generously. Sprinkle center of 15 cookies with slivered almonds.

Sprinkle gelatin on ¼ cup cold water to soften; stir over hot water until completely dissolved; cool. In medium bowl, with electric mixer at high speed, beat cooled gelatin with cocoa, cream and vanilla until soft peaks form. In another bowl, beat egg whites until foamy; beat in 6 tablespoons sugar, one tablespoonful at a time, beating until stiff peaks form. Fold into cocoa-cream mixture; refrigerate.

To serve: Spread each cookie without almonds with 3 tablespoons cocoa-cream mixture; top each with almond-topped cookie. Makes 15.

LEMON-CHIFFON CHOCOLATE TARTS
pictured between pages 112-113

Early in day: Preheat oven to 375° F. On floured surface, roll *half of reserved dough from Swedish Double-Chocolate Rounds,* above, into ¼-inch-thick round. With floured 4-inch round cookie cutter, cut out 5 circles. Carefully fit each circle over the outside of an ungreased 3¼-inch fluted tart pan. Repeat with other half of reserved dough.

Reroll any trimmings to get 2 more 4-inch circles to fit over tart pans. Bake the 12 tart shells, pastry side up, on cookie sheet 15 minutes, or until light brown. Cool; carefully remove shells from pans, pressing metal edges of pans in at top to loosen shells. Place on rack.

In small saucepan over low heat, stirring constantly, melt 6 ounces (*1½ bars*) *sweet cooking chocolate in 3 tablespoons water.* Brush inside of each tart generously with melted chocolate. Set aside.

About 1 hour 15 minutes before serving: Prepare one 3-ounce package lemon-flavor chiffon-pie filling as label directs. Pile lightly in tart shells. Grate 2 ounces (*remaining ½ bar*) *sweet cooking chocolate.* Sprinkle over tarts. Refrigerate. Makes 12 servings.

CHOCOLATE FRUIT COOKIES
pictured between pages 112-113

¾ cup butter or margarine
¾ cup granulated sugar
1 egg
⅓ cup shredded coconut
2½ cups all-purpose flour,
sifted before measuring
½ teaspoon vanilla extract
2 16-ounce cans cling-peach slices
2 tablespoons cornstarch
1 4-ounce bar sweet cooking chocolate
9 cooked prunes, pitted and halved
10 strawberries
1 cup finely chopped walnuts

Day before: Preheat oven to 375° F. In large bowl, with electric mixer at low speed, cream butter with sugar until light and fluffy; beat in egg and coconut; mix well. Gradually beat in flour and vanilla. Turn out on floured surface; roll into 18″ by 12″ rectangle. Cut lengthwise into 6 equal strips; cut each strip into 6 equal pieces, making 36 pieces.

With spatula, carefully lift pieces to ungreased cookie sheets; bake 12 minutes, or until lightly browned. Cool on racks. Store, uncovered.

Early in day: Drain peaches, reserving 1 cup juice; set aside peaches. In small saucepan, blend a little of the reserved juice with cornstarch; gradually add remaining juice, stirring until smooth. Cook over medium heat, stirring, until peach glaze is clear and thickened; cool.

In small saucepan over low heat, stirring constantly, melt chocolate in 2 tablespoons water. Brush cookies with chocolate; top each with a peach slice and a prune or strawberry half as pictured; coat with peach glaze; sprinkle edges with nuts. Makes 36.

SNOW CONES
pictured between pages 112-113

2 eggs
¾ cup granulated sugar
¾ cup all-purpose flour,
sifted before measuring
2 teaspoons grated lemon peel
2 teaspoons lemon juice
2 2-ounce packages whipped-topping mix
16 candied red cherries for garnish

Day before: Preheat oven to 375° F. In small bowl, with electric mixer at medium speed, beat eggs and sugar until light and lemon-colored. Gradually add flour, lemon peel and juice, beating just until smooth. Drop by heaping tablespoonfuls onto well-greased and floured cookie sheet; with spatula, spread batter into thin circle 5 inches in diameter. (Bake 3 or 4 circles at a time. Cones must be shaped quickly after baking, or circles will be too stiff to work with.)

Bake 6 to 8 minutes, or until circles are golden around edges. Using a pancake turner, loosen one circle from cookie sheet, leaving remaining circles on cookie sheet in oven, with the oven door left open. Holding the circle gently in both hands, quickly bring the two sides toward the center, overlapping enough to form a closed tip at bottom and a wide mouth at the top for filling. Cool cone, seam side down, on rack. Quickly shape remaining baked circles.

Continue to bake and shape cones as above with remaining batter; use a freshly prepared cookie sheet each time. Store, loosely covered.

About 10 minutes before serving: Prepare topping mixes, one at a time, as label directs. Place cones, open end up, in bowl. Fill with whipped topping and garnish with a cherry as pictured. Makes about 16 servings.

Note: For our pictured version, double the recipe.

COCONUT-MACAROON FUDGIES

Early in day: Preheat oven to 375° F. Slice *one 18-ounce roll refrigerated chocolate-chip slice-and-bake cookies* into ¾-inch-thick slices; cut each slice into quarters. Pat each quarter of dough around a candy kiss from *one 10-ounce package chocolate candy kisses,* rolling cookie between palms to make smooth ball that completely covers the candy kiss. In small bowl, place *one 4-ounce can flaked coconut.* Roll each cookie in coconut, patting coconut on to cover generously.

Place cookies about 2 inches apart on ungreased cookie sheets. Bake 8 to 10 minutes until golden. Cool slightly on cookie sheets; remove to racks to cool completely. Makes about 3½ dozen cookies.

PINEAPPLE-SPICE UPSIDE-DOWN CAKE

1¼ cups all-purpose flour,
sifted before measuring
1 teaspoon cinnamon
⅛ teaspoon ground cloves
½ teaspoon nutmeg
2 teaspoons double-acting baking powder
¼ teaspoon salt
3 tablespoons butter or margarine
½ cup packed brown sugar
1 15¼-ounce can pineapple chunks
5 maraschino cherries
⅓ cup shortening
½ cup granulated sugar
1 egg
1 teaspoon vanilla extract

is for Upside-down cakes and their luscious surprises

About 1½ hours before serving: Preheat oven to 350° F. Sift flour with cinnamon, cloves, nutmeg, baking powder and salt. Set aside.

In an 8-inch square baking pan, melt butter; sprinkle with brown sugar. Drain pineapple, reserving ½ cup of the syrup. On brown sugar and butter, arrange 6 pineapple chunks in a circle to form a small daisy; repeat, making 5 daisies in all. (Extra chunks may be placed between daisies and around edges of pan.) Place a cherry in the center of each daisy.

In large bowl, with electric mixer at medium speed, beat shortening and granulated sugar until creamy; add egg and vanilla; continue to beat until light and fluffy, about 4 minutes. With mixer at low speed, alternately beat in flour mixture and reserved pineapple syrup, just until smooth. Spread batter in pan, being careful to keep daisies intact. Bake 1 hour, or until cake tester inserted in center comes out clean. Cool in pan, on rack, 10 minutes.

With spatula, loosen cake from sides of pan. Invert serving plate over pan, then, with one hand under pan and the other over plate, turn both over so cake rests, fruit side up, on serving plate. Remove pan. If any fruit sticks to pan, lift off with spatula and put back in place on cake. Serve cake warm, topped with cream, whipped cream or vanilla ice cream if desired. Makes 6 to 8 servings.

◄§ PEACH: *Substitute one 16-ounce can peach slices or halves and ½ cup their syrup for pineapple chunks and syrup.*

◄§ CHERRY: *Substitute one 16-ounce can pitted red cherries, packed in water, drained, and ½ cup milk for pineapple chunks and syrup.*

DOUBLE FUDGE SQUARE

1 cup chocolate-flavored syrup
8 marshmallows, quartered
½ cup walnuts
1 18½-ounce package
chocolate-cake mix

About 1 hour before serving: Preheat oven to 350° F. In 2-cup measure, combine chocolate syrup with 1 cup water; pour into 8-inch square baking pan; sprinkle with marshmallows and nuts. Set aside.

Prepare cake mix as label directs; pour half the batter over the syrup mixture. Bake 35 to 45 minutes. (Remaining cake mix may be baked as cupcakes or as layer for dessert another day.)

To serve: Cut into squares; with wide spatula, serve upside down as is, or with light cream. Makes 6 servings.

CHOCOLATE-PINEAPPLE UPSIDE-DOWN CAKE

1 cup cake flour, sifted before measuring
¼ teaspoon salt
½ teaspoon baking soda
granulated sugar
¼ cup shortening
1 egg, lightly beaten
½ teaspoon vanilla extract
6 tablespoons milk
1 1-ounce square unsweetened chocolate, melted
3 tablespoons butter
1 15¼-ounce can sliced pineapple

About 2 hours before serving: Preheat oven to 350° F. Sift flour with salt, baking soda and ⅔ cup sugar. In large bowl, with spoon, cream shortening. Add flour mixture, egg, vanilla and milk; stir until flour is dampened. Blend in chocolate; beat vigorously for 1 minute.

Melt butter in 8-inch square metal cake pan; add ¼ cup sugar; over low heat, stir until butter and sugar are well blended. Lay halved pineapple slices on butter mixture. Pour on batter. Bake 45 minutes, or until cake tester inserted in center comes out clean. Cool in pan, on rack, 10 minutes.

Loosen cake with spatula and turn out on serving dish, pineapple side up. Serve warm, as is, or with whipped cream or vanilla ice cream. Makes 8 servings.

APPLE-MACAROON TURN-IT-OVER

⅔ cup butter or margarine
2 cups all-purpose flour,
sifted before measuring
5 medium, tart cooking apples
½ 8-ounce package
coconut macaroons, crumbled (1 cup)
¼ cup seedless raisins
1 cup packaged dried bread crumbs
¾ cup granulated sugar
1 teaspoon grated lemon peel
½ teaspoon cinnamon
¼ teaspoon nutmeg
1 teaspoon vanilla extract
confectioners' sugar
heavy or whipping cream

About 3 hours before serving: In large bowl, with pastry blender or 2 knives used scissor-fashion, cut butter into flour until mixture resembles coarse crumbs. Add 3 to 4 tablespoons cold water and quickly toss together until mixture forms smooth ball of pastry. Wrap in waxed paper; refrigerate.

Meanwhile, peel and core apples; thinly slice into large bowl. Add crumbled macaroons and raisins; toss lightly. In small bowl, mix the dried bread crumbs with granulated sugar, lemon peel, cinnamon, nutmeg and vanilla; add to apple mixture; toss well.

On lightly floured surface, with stockinette-covered rolling pin, roll chilled pastry into 17-inch circle; use rolling pin to help lift pastry into greased 1½-quart round glass casserole; gently ease pastry down into dish, letting pastry hang over sides. If pastry tears, mend by pressing edges together; or press piece of pastry gently over tear.

Preheat oven to 350° F. Fill pastry-lined casserole with apple mixture, lightly pressing apples down to eliminate any air spaces. To make top crust, fold overhanging pastry up over filling, overlapping it slightly in center; pat down edges firmly to seal. With tines of fork, prick top of pastry several times so steam will be able to escape. Bake pie 1 hour 50 minutes, or until bottom crust is golden brown. Cool on rack just until warm.

To serve: With small spatula, gently loosen sides of "Turn-It-Over." Place serving dish over top of casserole; invert casserole and serving dish together, then lift off casserole (there may be a slight indentation in center). Dust top generously with confectioners' sugar. Serve warm or cold, cut into wedges, with cream passed in pitcher, or whipped. Makes 8 servings.

GINGER-PEAR CAKE

About 1 hour before serving: Preheat oven to 375° F. In 9-inch square cake pan, melt ¼ *cup butter or margarine;* blend in *1 cup packed brown sugar.* Arrange one *29-ounce can pear halves,* drained, on top. Prepare one *13½-ounce package gingerbread mix* as label directs; pour over pears. Bake 40 minutes. Cool on rack 10 minutes. Turn out onto serving dish, pear side up. Serve warm, cut into squares with *whipped cream* or *vanilla ice cream.* Makes 9 servings.

BLUEBERRY PUFFS

1 tablespoon lemon juice
2 cups fresh or partially thawed
frozen blueberries
1 cup all-purpose flour,
sifted before measuring
2 teaspoons double-acting baking powder
¼ teaspoon salt
2 tablespoons shortening
½ cup granulated sugar
1 egg
½ teaspoon lemon extract
¼ cup milk

About 1 hour before serving: Preheat oven to 400° F. Sprinkle juice on berries; spoon into six greased 6-ounce custard cups. Sift flour with baking powder and salt. In bowl, with spoon, cream shortening; slowly add sugar, beating until light; beat in egg and extract. Add milk and flour mixture all at once; stir just until blended. Spoon over berries. Bake ½ hour or until done. Cool on rack 10 minutes; turn out, berry side up, on plates. Serve with cream, if desired. Makes 6 servings.

APPLE UPSIDE-DOWN GINGERBREAD

About 45 minutes before serving: Preheat oven as label of one *13½-ounce package of gingerbread mix* directs. In 9-inch square cake pan, melt *2 tablespoons butter or margarine;* blend in ¼ *cup packed light brown sugar;* spread evenly in bottom of pan; top with *1 large unpeeled cooking apple* cut into ½-inch-thick slices. Set aside.

Prepare gingerbread mix as label directs; pour evenly over apple slices. Bake as label directs, or until cake tester inserted in center comes out clean. Cool in pan, on rack, 10 minutes; invert onto serving plate. Serve warm or cold with *whipped cream.* Makes 9 servings.

Mock Alaska Pancake Torte, page 150, a party dessert without equal

A luxurious layer of almond paste covers this White Fruitcake, page 158

A very special ending for a very special party, Venetian Rum Cake, page 166

From the pastry cart: Twin Petits Fours, page 169, and Easy Petits Fours, page 168

VACHERIN
pictured between pages 112-113

10 egg whites at room temperature
½ teaspoon cream of tartar
½ teaspoon salt
3 cups granulated sugar
2 teaspoons vanilla extract
Strawberry Cream (below)

is for Vacherin
plus more
marvelous meringues

Four days before serving: On heavy brown paper, draw, then cut out, one 7-inch circle and five 8-inch circles. On each of two large cookie sheets, place 3 of these paper circles. Preheat oven to 225° F.

In large bowl, with electric mixer at high speed, beat 5 of the egg whites until foamy; beat in ¼ teaspoon each cream of tartar and salt. Continuing to beat, gradually add ¾ cup of the sugar, beating to a stiff meringue. Fold in 1 teaspoon vanilla and another ¾ cup sugar.

Place a number 6 tube in large pastry bag; fill with meringue. On four of the 8-inch circles, using outer edge as a guide, pipe ring of meringue about 1 inch wide. On fifth 8-inch circle, pipe ring in exactly the same way, then continue piping smaller and smaller rings until circle is covered. This solid ring becomes the Vacherin base. For lid, fill in 7-inch circle as you did circle for base. Wash pastry bag and tube; set aside to dry. Bake all meringues 45 minutes; turn off oven and leave meringues in oven 2 hours to dry. Remove paper from the four 8-inch rings, but not from base or lid.

Make up second batch of meringue, using 5 remaining egg whites with rest of the cream of tartar, salt, sugar and vanilla as above. On cookie sheet, place Vacherin base; spread top edge with meringue, then top with one of meringue rings. Repeat, spreading meringue and adding rings until the four rings are used and you have a "bowl."

Completely cover outside of "bowl" with meringue, smoothing it on with spatula. With same pastry bag and tube filled with meringue, make design (we made large S's) around outside of "bowl." Press out row of rosettes around base. Preheat oven to 225° F.

Next, cover the 7-inch lid with rows of rosettes, as pictured. Use remaining meringue, if any, to smooth out inside of "bowl." Place lid and "bowl" on cookie sheet. Bake 45 minutes; turn off oven and leave in oven at least 2 hours to dry. With spatula, loosen carefully and peel off paper. Store in dry, airy place until ready to use; do not store in tightly covered container.

Just before serving: Make Strawberry-Cream filling. Spoon into "bowl"; cover with lid; serve right away. Makes 10 to 12 servings.

❧ STRAWBERRY CREAM: In bowl, combine *2 cups heavy or whipping cream, whipped with 1 cup drained, thawed, frozen sliced strawberries and ¼ teaspoon almond extract.*

AFTER-DINNER MERINGUES

6 egg whites at room temperature
⅛ teaspoon cream of tartar
1½ cups granulated sugar
½ teaspoon vanilla extract
red or green food color
flaked coconut or sugar confetti for garnish

Early in day: Preheat oven to 200° F. In large bowl, with electric mixer at high speed, beat egg whites until foamy; beat in cream of tartar until soft peaks form. Slowly add sugar, continuing to beat until sugar is dissolved, about 15 minutes. Add vanilla and few drops of food color. Continue beating until meringue is glossy and forms stiff peaks.

On large, greased cookie sheet, using a number 20 ice-cream scoop, place balls of meringue about 1½ to 2 inches apart. Sprinkle with a little coconut or confetti. Bake 4 hours or until very crisp and dry. Cool on cookie sheet away from drafts. Makes 12 servings.

MERINGUE MELBA

1 30-ounce can cling-peach halves
1 10-ounce package frozen raspberries, thawed
¾ teaspoon almond extract
4 egg whites
⅛ teaspoon cream of tartar
¼ cup granulated sugar

Early in day or about 1½ hours before serving: Drain 6 peach halves; set aside (reserve any leftover peach halves for use another day) .

Drain raspberries well, reserving juice. In covered electric-blender container at low speed, blend raspberries and almond extract until smooth; if necessary, stir in enough reserved juice to make ¾ cup. (Or in small bowl, with fork, vigorously stir and mash berries until well blended and slightly smooth.) Into each of six 5-ounce custard cups, place 1 tablespoon raspberry mixture; top with peach half, cut side up; spoon 1 tablespoon raspberry mixture over each peach.

Preheat oven to 425° F. In small bowl, with electric mixer at high speed, beat egg whites until foamy. Add cream of tartar and continue beating until soft peaks form. Gradually add sugar, beating until sugar is dissolved and meringue forms stiff peaks. Spoon meringue over fruit in custard cups, spreading it to edges of cups and mounding it in the center. Place on cookie sheet; bake 2 to 3 minutes until meringue is lightly browned. Cool; refrigerate. Makes 6 servings.

MERINGUE-TOPPED PINEAPPLE CAKE

4 egg whites at room temperature
1½ cups granulated sugar
1¾ cups all-purpose flour,
sifted before measuring
2¼ teaspoons double-acting baking powder
¾ teaspoon salt
½ cup butter or margarine
⅔ cup milk
1 teaspoon vanilla extract
2 eggs
grated peel of 1 lemon
2 tablespoons sliced blanched almonds
Pineapple Filling (below)
2 2-ounce packages whipped-topping mix
1 tablespoon slivered toasted almonds
for garnish

Early in day: Grease and flour two 9-inch layer-cake pans. Set aside.

In small bowl, with electric mixer at high speed, beat egg whites until foamy; add ¾ cup of the sugar, 2 tablespoons at a time, beating until very stiff peaks form, about 10 minutes. Set meringue aside.

Preheat oven to 350° F. Sift flour with baking powder and salt.

In large bowl, with electric mixer at medium speed, cream butter with remaining ¾ cup sugar. Gradually beat in, alternately, flour mixture with milk and vanilla. Add eggs, one at a time, beating well after each addition, then beat in lemon peel. Pour into prepared pans. Spread meringue over batter, ⅛ inch in from edge of pans. Sprinkle blanched almonds in ring on top. Bake 35 to 45 minutes or until cake tester inserted in center of layers comes out clean.

Cool in pans, on rack, 10 minutes. With spatula, carefully loosen cake from pans; remove layers, meringue side up; cool on racks.

Prepare Pineapple Filling; spread between cake layers. Refrigerate 1 hour or until filling is cool.

Prepare topping mixes, one at a time, as label directs. Spread on sides of cake; garnish with toasted almonds. Chill. Makes 10 servings.

৵§ PINEAPPLE FILLING: *In double-boiler top, mix 2 tablespoons granulated sugar, 4 teaspoons cornstarch, ¼ teaspoon salt; add 2 egg yolks, slightly beaten. With wire whisk, stir in ⅔ cup milk. Cook over boiling water, stirring constantly, until thickened. Fold in two 8½-ounce cans crushed pineapple, well drained, 1 tablespoon butter or margarine and 1½ teaspoons lemon juice. Mix well.*

WAFFLES À LA MODE

2 cups all-purpose flour,
sifted before measuring
4 teaspoons double-acting baking powder
1 teaspoon salt
2 cups milk
4 eggs, separated
1 cup melted butter or margarine
ice cream
chocolate sauce

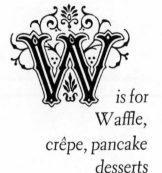

*is for
Waffle,
crêpe, pancake
desserts*

About 10 minutes before baking: Preheat waffle baker as manufacturer directs. Into large bowl, sift flour, baking powder and salt. With electric mixer at high speed, beat in milk and egg yolks until batter is smooth; stir in butter. In another large bowl, with electric mixer at high speed, beat egg whites until stiff; fold into batter.

To bake, pour batter evenly over waffle baker until it spreads to about 1 inch from edges. Bake as manufacturer directs. Do not raise cover until waffle is done. Loosen waffle with fork. Serve at once with ice cream and sauce. Reheat iron before baking the next waffle. Makes 6 to 8 servings.

CAKE-MIX BELGIAN WAFFLES

3 pints fresh strawberries
confectioners' sugar
4 eggs, separated
1 18½-ounce package yellow-cake mix
2½ cups heavy or whipping cream
½ teaspoon salt

About 1 hour ahead: Slice fresh strawberries; if desired, sprinkle with confectioners' sugar; refrigerate.

About ½ hour before serving: Heat waffle baker as manufacturer directs. With electric mixer at high speed, beat egg whites until they stand in stiff peaks when beater is raised; set aside.

In large bowl, combine egg yolks, cake mix, 1½ cups of the cream and salt; blend, then beat, at medium speed, 2 minutes. Fold in beaten whites. Bake as manufacturer directs or until steaming stops and waffle is golden; remove. Reheat baker before making next waffle.

Serve two hot waffle sections, one atop the other. Sprinkle each with confectioners' sugar, and top with some sliced strawberries and rest of cream, whipped. Makes 12 servings.

CHERRY WAFFLES CHÂTELAINE

1 16-ounce can pitted dark sweet cherries
1 16-ounce can light sweet cherries
1 cup granulated sugar
2 tablespoons grated orange peel
red food color
3 tablespoons cornstarch
8 frozen waffles
vanilla ice cream

About 20 minutes before serving: Drain cherries, reserving juice.

In large skillet, combine cherry juices, sugar, orange peel and a few drops food color. In small bowl, add enough juice mixture to cornstarch to make a smooth paste; stir back into juice mixture. Bring to boiling, stirring; cook until clear and thickened; stir in cherries.

Meanwhile, heat waffles as package label directs. Top each waffle with ice cream; cover with hot cherry sauce. Makes 8 servings.

STRAWBERRY DESSERT OMELET

4 eggs, separated
¼ teaspoon cream of tartar
3 tablespoons granulated sugar
¼ teaspoon salt
2 tablespoons butter or margarine
2 cups sliced strawberries
confectioners' sugar

About ½ hour before serving: Preheat oven to 350° F. In large bowl, with electric mixer at high speed, beat egg whites until foamy; add cream of tartar and continue beating until stiff peaks form.

In small bowl, with electric mixer at high speed, beat yolks with ¼ cup cold water, 2 tablespoons of the granulated sugar and salt until very light and fluffy; carefully fold into beaten whites.

Heat butter in 10-inch ovenproof skillet; pour in egg mixture; cook, without stirring, 3 minutes or until puffy and golden on underside when lifted with spatula. Without turning, place in oven; bake for 10 minutes or until top springs back when lightly touched and is golden.

Meanwhile, in bowl, toss berries with remaining tablespoon sugar.

Run spatula around sides to loosen omelet. With knife, make crease across center of omelet; spoon berries on one side of crease; tip skillet, and with wide spatula, fold omelet in half; slide onto warm plate. Sprinkle with confectioners' sugar. Serve immediately. Makes 4 servings.

MOCK ALASKA PANCAKE TORTE
pictured between pages 144-145

2 cups all-purpose flour,
sifted before measuring
4 teaspoons double-acting baking powder
salt
8 eggs, separated
2 teaspoons vanilla extract
granulated sugar
melted butter or margarine
2½ cups milk
1½ cups creamed cottage cheese
1 egg yolk
1 tablespoon grated lemon peel
4 egg whites
¼ teaspoon cream of tartar
¼ cup apricot preserves
1½ 1-ounce squares
semisweet chocolate, grated

Early in day: Sift flour with baking powder and ¼ teaspoon salt. In large bowl, with electric mixer at medium speed, blend 8 of the egg yolks with vanilla and ¼ cup sugar; gradually beat in flour mixture alternately with ½ cup melted butter and milk. Refrigerate 1 hour.

In large bowl, with electric mixer at high speed, beat 8 of the egg whites with a dash of salt until stiff; fold into chilled batter.

Onto hot, well-greased 10-inch skillet, pour 1 cup of batter, tilting pan to spread batter. Cook slowly until top is covered with bubbles and edges look cooked; turn with broad spatula and cook other side until golden. Repeat until all batter is used; cool, then stack with waxed paper between pancakes. Wrap in foil; refrigerate.

About 1 hour before serving: Cream cottage cheese with ¼ cup sugar, 1 egg yolk and lemon peel; set aside. Preheat oven to 450° F.

In medium bowl, with electric mixer at high speed, beat 4 egg whites with dash of salt and cream of tartar until foamy; add ½ cup sugar gradually, beating well after each addition; beat until stiff.

On lightly greased 12-inch pizza pan or cookie sheet, place 1 of the pancakes; spread evenly with half of cottage-cheese mixture. Top with another pancake; spread with 2 tablespoons apricot preserves. Top with another pancake; sprinkle with half of grated chocolate and 2 teaspoons melted butter. Repeat layers, using all fillings and 3 more pancakes; top with a seventh pancake to complete the torte.

Completely frost with meringue, swirling with spoon or spatula into peaks on top. Bake 3 minutes, or until light brown. Cut into wedges. Makes 8 to 10 servings.

ELEGANT DESSERT CRÊPES

⅔ cup all-purpose flour,
sifted before measuring
1 tablespoon granulated sugar
¼ teaspoon salt
2 eggs, slightly beaten
1½ cups milk
butter or margarine
vanilla extract
2 10-ounce packages frozen mixed fruit
in quick-thaw pouches
1 cup heavy or whipping cream

Day before: Sift flour with sugar and salt. In medium bowl, combine eggs, milk, 1 tablespoon melted butter and a drop of vanilla. With rotary beater, beat until well blended. Add flour all at once; beat well. Pour batter into large glass measuring cup. Chill about 2 hours.

In 6-inch skillet, heat 1 teaspoon butter until very hot, but not brown; pour in ¼ cup batter, tilting pan quickly so batter covers bottom. Cook over medium heat until top is set and underside is brown. With broad spatula, carefully lift crêpe and flip it over; cook a few minutes more to brown other side. Place crêpe on piece of waxed paper; regrease skillet and continue making crêpes, stacking them between waxed paper until batter is used up; cover; refrigerate.

Just before serving: Separate crêpes and let come to room temperature. Thaw fruit as label directs. Whip cream until stiff, sweetening if desired; place a heaping tablespoonful on edge of crêpe, fold up, cornucopia fashion. Arrange filled crêpes in ring on serving dish; drain fruit; spoon it into center of crêpes. Makes 6 servings.

THIN, LIGHT AND SWEET PANCAKES

1¾ cups of 8½-ounce package
poundcake mix
1 cup milk
1 egg
melted butter or margarine
confectioners' sugar
sweetened fresh or thawed frozen,
sliced strawberries

About 45 minutes before serving: In large bowl, combine poundcake mix, milk, egg and 2 tablespoons melted butter; with rotary beater, beat until batter is smooth. Into hot, lightly buttered 10-inch skillet, pour ¼ cup batter. Cook until top is covered with bubbles and edges look cooked; turn with broad spatula; cook until underside is golden. Repeat until all the batter is used. Keep pancakes warm on foil-covered cookie sheet in 200° F. oven.

To serve: Sprinkle hot pancakes with confectioners' sugar. Place two pancakes on each plate; top with some sliced berries. Makes about 10 pancakes or 5 servings.

ORANGE-MINCE CRÊPES

3 eggs
¾ cup milk
½ teaspoon salad oil
1½ cups packaged buttermilk-biscuit mix
dash salt
butter or margarine
1 cup prepared mincemeat
¼ cup sherry
12 long, thin slivers of orange peel
¼ cup orange juice
2 tablespoons slivered almonds

1. *Early in day:* In covered electric-blender container, or in large bowl with rotary beater, mix eggs, milk, salad oil, biscuit mix and salt with ¾ cup water until smooth and well blended.
2. In 7-inch skillet over medium heat, heat ½ teaspoon butter until bubbly; heat another 7-inch or slightly larger skillet with another ½ teaspoon butter. Into first skillet, using ¼-cup measuring cup as dipper, pour ¼ cup of the crêpe batter; quickly tip or "roll" pan until batter coats bottom and extends up sides. When top is dry and underside golden, turn crêpe into other hot buttered skillet to brown other side; invert crêpe onto paper toweling; cool. Repeat until 12 crêpes are made and cooled. Stack with waxed paper between each; wrap in foil; chill.*
3. *About ½ hour before serving:* Remove crêpes from refrigerator; unwrap.

In small saucepan, heat mincemeat with sherry, orange peel and juice; toss in almonds; keep warm over low heat.
4. In large skillet, melt 2 tablespoons butter; fold each crêpe into quarters and place in skillet; heat through, turning often. When hot, turn heat off; arrange crêpes in curved row down center of skillet. Spoon mincemeat sauce on either side of crêpes. Serve from skillet, spooning some sauce over each serving. Makes 6 servings.

*Crepes may be freezer-wrapped and frozen up to 1 week ahead. To serve, let thaw at room temperature 3 hours. Heat in sauce as above.

STRAWBERRY PANCAKES

3 cups sliced strawberries
3 tablespoons granulated sugar
1 3-ounce package cream cheese, softened
1 cup heavy or whipping cream
packaged pancake mix
butter or margarine
confectioners' sugar

About 1 hour before serving: Toss berries with granulated sugar. Chill.

In small bowl, with electric mixer at medium speed, beat cheese until creamy; slowly beat in cream until thick, but not stiff; chill.

Prepare pancake batter as label directs for 12 to 14 thinner pancakes. In 7-inch skillet, melt a little butter; pour in ¼ cup batter, tilting pan to spread batter; cook until top is covered with bubbles and edges look cooked; with spatula, turn to cook other side. Repeat until all batter is used. Meanwhile, keep pancakes warm on foil-covered cookie sheet in 200° F. oven.

To serve: Place about ¼ cup sliced berries on each pancake; roll up and sprinkle with confectioners' sugar; garnish with remaining berries; top each with some of the cheese mixture. Makes 6 to 8 servings.

AMBROSIA PANCAKES

½ cup packaged pancake mix
1¼ cups milk
1 egg
2 tablespoons melted butter or margarine
2 teaspoons almond extract
2 teaspoons granulated sugar
1 cup flaked coconut
1 20-ounce can pineapple chunks,
lightly drained

About 45 minutes before serving: In bowl, combine pancake mix, milk, egg, butter, extract, sugar and ⅔ cup of the coconut; beat until well blended. Onto hot, well-greased 8-inch skillet, pour about ¼ cup of the batter. Cook until top is covered with bubbles and edges look cooked. Turn with broad spatula; cook on other side until golden. Repeat, stirring batter well each time before pouring, making 8 pancakes in all. Keep warm on foil-covered cookie sheet in 200° F. oven.

To serve: Top each pancake with a chunk or two of pineapple, sprinkled with some of remaining coconut. Makes 8 servings.

WALNUT DESSERT PANCAKES

2 cups packaged buttermilk-biscuit mix
1 egg
1¾ cups milk
1 cup coarsely chopped walnuts
butter or margarine
1 quart vanilla ice cream
1 11-ounce jar caramel topping

About 1 hour before serving: In large bowl, combine biscuit mix, egg and milk; with rotary beater, beat until smooth; stir in walnuts. In well-buttered, hot, 7-inch skillet, pour ¼ cup of the batter; cook over medium heat until top is covered with bubbles and edges look cooked. Turn over with broad spatula; cook until underside is golden. Repeat with rest of batter, keeping pancakes warm on foil-covered cookie sheet in 200° F. oven.

To serve: Top each pancake with vanilla ice cream and caramel topping. Makes about 14 pancakes.

ICE-CREAM PANCAKELETS

½ cup all-purpose flour
½ teaspoon double-acting baking powder
¼ teaspoon baking soda
1 tablespoon granulated sugar
1 cup sour cream
½ cup heavy or whipping cream
2 eggs, separated
2 tablespoons melted butter
1 pint ice cream
maple syrup

About 1 hour before serving: Sift flour with next 3 ingredients. In medium bowl, slowly stir creams together until smooth; stir in slightly beaten egg yolks, then butter; gradually blend in flour mixture.

In small bowl, with electric mixer at high speed, beat egg whites until stiff; fold into flour mixture until batter is smooth.

Onto well-greased hot skillet or griddle, drop heaping tablespoons of batter. Cook over low heat until top is covered with bubbles; turn with spatula; cook underside until golden. Repeat until batter is used. Keep pancakes warm on foil-covered cookie sheet in 200° F. oven.

To serve: Place 3 or 4 pancakes, overlapping, on each dessert plate; top with some ice cream; drizzle with syrup. Makes 6 servings.

RHUBARB-CREAM DESSERT CRÊPES

12 crêpes, at room temperature
1½ pounds rhubarb cut into 1-inch pieces
granulated sugar
⅛ teaspoon salt
1 tablespoon cornstarch
1 3-ounce package cream cheese, softened
1 cup heavy or whipping cream

About 2 hours before serving: Prepare crêpes from your favorite recipe or as in steps 1 and 2 Orange-Mince Crêpes (page 152). Do not chill.

In medium saucepan, combine rhubarb, ½ cup sugar, 2 tablespoons water and salt. Simmer 5 minutes, or until rhubarb is tender. In cup, blend cornstarch with 1 tablespoon water until smooth; gradually stir into rhubarb; cook, stirring, until slightly thickened. Refrigerate.

In small bowl, with electric mixer at medium speed, beat cream cheese until smooth; slowly beat in cream and 1 teaspoon sugar until mixture is smooth, but not stiff.

To serve: Place heaping tablespoon of cream-cheese mixture in center of each crêpe. Top with about 3 tablespoons rhubarb. Fold edges of crêpe around filling to make a cornucopia. Makes 12 servings.

SPICY DESSERT PANCAKES

2 cups packaged buttermilk-biscuit mix
1 package active dry yeast
1 cup milk
1 egg
1 16-ounce can raspberry applesauce
½ teaspoon cinnamon
¼ teaspoon ground cloves
nutmeg
½ teaspoon almond extract
sour cream

About 45 minutes before serving: In large bowl, blend biscuit mix and yeast. In small saucepan, heat milk with ⅔ cup water until very warm; gradually stir into biscuit mixture. With electric mixer at low speed, beat 1 minute; add egg and beat 1 minute longer. Cover with foil and let stand at room temperature ½ hour.

Meanwhile, in bowl, combine applesauce, cinnamon, cloves, ¼ teaspoon nutmeg and almond extract; set aside.

About 15 minutes before serving: Stir down batter. Onto hot, lightly greased griddle or skillet, pour ¼ cup batter. Cook over medium heat, until top is covered with bubbles and edges look cooked. With broad spatula, turn and cook underside until golden. Repeat with remaining batter, keeping pancakes warm on foil-covered cookie sheet in 200° F. oven.

To serve: On one half of each pancake, place heaping tablespoon of the applesauce mixture, then fold other half over it. Arrange filled pancakes on warm serving platter. Serve with bowl of sour cream sprinkled with nutmeg to be spooned over the pancakes, if desired. Makes 6 servings of about 3 pancakes each.

LITTLE CHOCOLATE PANCAKE TORTES

1 4-ounce package sweet cooking chocolate
¼ cup warm milk
packaged pancake mix
granulated sugar
butter or margarine
1 cup heavy or whipping cream
½ cup flaked coconut
8 large fresh strawberries

Early in day: Break chocolate into small chunks; place in 1-cup glass measuring cup. Place cup in small saucepan of hot, *not boiling*, water, stirring constantly until chocolate is completely melted. Gradually stir in warm milk until well blended.

Prepare pancake batter as label directs for 10 to 12 pancakes; slowly blend in melted chocolate mixture and 1 tablespoon sugar.

Generously brush 10-inch skillet with butter; also brush inside of 2¾-inch round metal cookie cutter with butter. Place cookie cutter on hot skillet over medium heat; pour about 1 level measuring tablespoon of batter into cookie cutter, being sure batter spreads to touch all the way around.

When top of pancake shows bubbles and edges look cooked, with pot holder, lift off cookie cutter; set it on hot skillet in another spot and pour in 1 tablespoon batter; while it cooks, turn first pancake with broad spatula or pancake turner to brown underside. Repeat, cooking 3 pancakes at a time, until batter is used up, making about 32 pancakes.

About 20 minutes before serving: In bowl, with rotary beater, whip cream with 2 teaspoons sugar until soft peaks form. Spread 1 heaping teaspoonful on each pancake; stack 4 pancakes on each serving plate. Top each stack with sprinkling of coconut and a strawberry. Makes 8 servings.

SPRINGERLE

anise seed
4½ cups all-purpose flour,
sifted before measuring
1 teaspoon double-acting baking powder
4 eggs
1 pound confectioners' sugar
1 tablespoon grated lemon peel

Three weeks before serving: Grease cookie sheet; sprinkle with anise seed. Sift together flour and baking powder. In bowl, with electric mixer, beat eggs until light; add sugar; beat until well mixed. Add lemon peel, then flour mixture. Mix well. Chill 1 hour or until firm enough to handle easily.

On lightly floured surface, roll dough to ½-inch thickness. Flour springerle mold well; press firmly into dough; remove mold. Mark rest of dough in same way, flouring mold each time. With knife, cut cookies along border markings. Place on cookie sheet, ½ inch apart; leave exposed to air overnight.

About 15 minutes before baking: Preheat oven to 350° F. Bake cookies ½ hour or until done. Store, covered. Springerle keep for months. Makes 2½ dozen.

 is for *Xmas treats, from fruitcakes to cookies*

LEKERLIS

2 cups cake flour, sifted before measuring
¼ teaspoon salt
¼ teaspoon nutmeg
¾ cup granulated sugar
¼ cup honey
1 egg
1 cup ground almonds
1½ teaspoons grated lemon peel
⅓ cup finely cut candied
lemon and orange peel

Two to 4 weeks before serving: Sift flour with salt and nutmeg. In large bowl, thoroughly mix sugar and honey with egg. Stir in almonds and lemon peel; mix well. Blend in flour mixture; mix well. Chill 1 hour or until firm enough to roll easily.

Preheat oven to 350° F. On lightly floured surface, roll dough to ⅛-inch thickness. Cut into 2-inch rounds. Place on greased cookie sheet; bake 10 to 12 minutes or until done. Store, tightly covered. Lekerlis keep for months. Makes 5 dozen.

WHITE FRUITCAKE
pictured between pages 144-145

¾ pound pecan or walnut meats,
coarsely chopped (3 cups)
2 8-ounce jars candied pineapple,
coarsely diced
¾ pound citron, diced (about 2 cups)
2 8-ounce jars candied cherries
2 cups all-purpose flour,
sifted before measuring
2 teaspoons double-acting baking powder
1 cup butter or margarine, softened
1 cup granulated sugar
5 eggs
1½ teaspoons rose water
½ cup sherry
Charleston Almond Paste (opposite)
White Icing (opposite)

Several weeks before serving: With brown paper, line 10-inch angel-cake pan; grease well. In bowl, combine nuts, pineapple, citron and cherries; sift flour and baking powder over all; toss until well mixed.

In deep 16-quart kettle, set wire rack on 3 inverted custard cups; add water just to top of rack; bring to boiling.

Meanwhile, in large bowl, with electric mixer at medium speed, beat butter and sugar until fluffy. Beat in eggs, one at a time, then rose water and sherry; fold into floured fruits and nuts. Spoon into lined cake pan. Completely wrap filled cake pan in 32″ by 18″ piece of heavy-duty foil; place on wire rack, adding enough boiling water to come 2 inches up side of wrapped cake pan. Cover; steam 3 hours. About 15 minutes before time is up, preheat oven to 325° F.

When cake is steamed, remove foil from pan; bake cake ½ hour or until cake tester inserted in center comes out clean. Cool on rack in pan; remove from pan; wrap in foil and refrigerate.

Meanwhile, make Charleston Almond Paste. When cake is chilled, remove foil and brown paper. On waxed paper, roll Almond Paste into 26″ by 8″ rectangle; cut crosswise into 4 even strips and use to completely cover top and sides of fruitcake, overlapping strips slightly on sides as well as at center top; pat paste snugly into cake. Wrap in plastic wrap or foil. Refrigerate until 2 days before serving.

Two days before serving: Make White Icing. Unwrap cake and spread icing completely over top and sides of almond-paste-coated cake. Refrigerate until serving time.

To serve: Cut into small wedges. Makes about 24 servings. Leftovers keep well if securely wrapped and refrigerated.

CHARLESTON ALMOND PASTE

Finely grind or blend in covered electric-blender container, *2 pounds blanched almonds.* In large bowl, with electric mixer at medium speed, beat *5 egg whites* with *2 pounds confectioners' sugar* until smooth. Add *2 teaspoons rose water* and *4 teaspoons almond extract.* Beat in almonds; when too stiff to beat, turn onto work surface, knead until smooth.

WHITE ICING

In saucepan over low heat, simmer *2 cups granulated sugar* with *1 cup water* to 234° F. on candy thermometer, or until mixture spins thread when dropped from spoon.

Meanwhile, in medium bowl, with electric mixer at medium speed, beat *2 egg whites* until soft peaks form. Gradually beat in half of sugar syrup (let other half continue to simmer slowly) until well blended. Beat in *3 tablespoons lemon juice* and *8 large marshmallows,* one at a time. Pour in other half of syrup, beating until stiff peaks form.

NO-BAKE PLUM PUDDING

2 3-ounce packages lemon-flavor gelatin
⅛ teaspoon salt
½ teaspoon ground cloves
1 teaspoon cinnamon
1½ cups finely chopped
dark seedless raisins
1½ cups finely chopped cooked prunes
1½ cups finely chopped walnuts
1½ cups grapenuts cereal
½ cup finely chopped citron
10 to 12 walnut halves for garnish
Custard Sauce (page 124)

Day before or early in day: In medium bowl, dissolve gelatin and salt in 2 cups boiling water. Add 2 cups cold water, cloves and cinnamon. Refrigerate until consistency of unbeaten egg whites, about 2 hours.

Fold in raisins, prunes, chopped walnuts, cereal and citron; spoon 2 to 3 tablespoons of this gelatin mixture into 2-quart mold; arrange walnut halves in circle on top. Refrigerate for 20 minutes or until almost set. Spoon on ¼ to ½ cup more of gelatin mixture, or enough to cover walnut halves. Refrigerate about 20 minutes or until almost set. Spoon in remaining gelatin mixture; refrigerate until firm.

To serve: Unmold; top with Custard Sauce. Makes 10 to 12 servings.

FATTIGMAND

3 eggs
3 tablespoons heavy or whipping cream
¼ cup granulated sugar
1½ tablespoons melted shortening
1 tablespoon brandy
½ teaspoon salt
½ teaspoon ground cardamom
about 3 cups all-purpose flour
salad oil
confectioners' sugar

Early in day: In bowl, mix eggs with cream and sugar. Blend in shortening, brandy, salt, cardamom and 2 cups of the flour. Stir in enough additional flour to make stiff dough. Wrap in waxed paper; chill.

In deep saucepan, heat 2 inches of salad oil to 365° F. on deep-fat thermometer. On lightly floured surface, roll half of chilled dough paper-thin. Cut into diamonds 3 inches long. Make slit in center of each; pull one corner through slit. Fry until delicate brown. Cool. Dust with confectioners' sugar. Repeat with rest of dough. Makes 96.

ORANGE-NUT CAKE

1 19-ounce package orange-cake mix
2 cups ricotta cheese
2 tablespoons milk
2 cups confectioners' sugar
¼ cup finely chopped fresh orange peel
¼ cup diced candied citron
¼ cup diced candied lemon peel
¼ cup rum (optional)
1 envelope unflavored gelatin
2 cups heavy or whipping cream
1 cup very coarsely chopped hazelnuts

Early in day: Prepare cake mix as label directs; bake in two 8-inch layer-cake pans. Cool on rack.

Meanwhile, in medium bowl with electric mixer at medium speed, beat cheese and milk until smooth. Gradually beat in 1½ cups of the sugar. Fold in orange peel, citron and lemon peel.

With sharp knife, split each layer in half horizontally, making 4 layers in all. Sprinkle each layer with 1 tablespoon of the rum if desired.

Place one layer on cake plate; spread with ⅓ of the cheese mixture. Repeat with 2 more layers, each spread with ⅓ of the cheese mixture; top with fourth layer. Refrigerate.

In measuring cup, sprinkle gelatin over ¼ cup cold water; place cup in pan of hot water; stir until dissolved; cool slightly.

In medium bowl, whip cream with remaining ½ cup sugar until fairly stiff. Add cooled gelatin; beat until stiff. Spread over cake; garnish with chopped nuts; chill. To cut, use warmed knife. Makes 10 servings.

HOLIDAY NESSELRODE PIE

1½ cups finely ground walnuts
granulated sugar
1 envelope plus 1 teaspoon
unflavored gelatin
1½ cups milk
½ teaspoon salt
6 eggs, separated
2 tablespoons rum or rum extract
2 teaspoons grated lemon peel
1 4-ounce jar diced mixed candied fruits
(about ½ cup)
2 2-ounce packages whipped-topping mix
1 slice candied green pineapple, slivered
¼ slice candied red pineapple, minced

Day before: Preheat oven to 400° F. In 10-inch pie plate, mix walnuts with 2 tablespoons sugar; with back of spoon, press mixture into plate to form pie shell. Bake 8 minutes or until lightly browned.

Meanwhile, in double-boiler top, soften gelatin in milk; add ¼ cup sugar, salt and slightly beaten egg yolks; stir until blended. Cook over hot, *not boiling*, water, stirring constantly, until mixture thickens slightly and coats spoon. Remove from heat; stir in rum and lemon peel. Place waxed paper directly on surface of mixture; chill until cool, but not firm.

In large bowl, with electric mixer at high speed, beat egg whites until foamy; gradually add ¼ cup sugar, beating until stiff but not dry. Into the egg-white mixture, gradually fold cooled gelatin mixture and candied fruits. Pile into pie shell; chill until firm.

To serve: Prepare topping mixes, one at a time, as label directs. Spread on pie; garnish with pineapple. Makes about 10 servings.

GRAHAM-CRACKER FRUITCAKE

2 cups dark seedless raisins
1 cup chopped walnuts
2 cups golden seedless raisins
1 cup pitted dates, chopped
½ cup halved candied cherries
⅔ cup slivered candied pineapple
¼ cup diced candied citron
⅓ cup slivered candied orange or lemon peel
port wine
1 tablespoon vanilla extract
1 cup butter or margarine, softened
1 cup granulated sugar
6 eggs
1½ 13¼-ounce packages
graham-cracker crumbs (4½ to 5 cups)
Glaze (below)

Two weeks or up to 1 month before serving: In large bowl, combine all fruits, nuts and peel with 1 cup port wine and vanilla. Cover tightly and let stand several days or at least overnight.

Preheat oven to 250° F. In large bowl, with electric mixer at medium speed, beat butter and sugar until creamy. Beat in eggs, two at a time, until well blended. Beat in graham-cracker crumbs alternately with fruit-nut mixture, including any wine that fruit hasn't absorbed, until thoroughly mixed.

Grease one 10-inch springform pan or two 9" by 5" loaf pans or one 10-inch tube pan. Line with waxed paper and grease again. Pour batter into pan. Bake 4 hours in springform pan, 3½ hours in loaf pans or tube pan, or until cake tester inserted in center comes out clean. Cool cake in pan on rack.

When cake is completely cooled, remove from pan and carefully peel off paper. Wrap fruitcake in cheesecloth and sprinkle liberally with port wine. Wrap tightly in foil or plastic wrap and store in cool place, sprinkling once a week with port wine. Store at least 2 weeks.

Several hours before serving: Brush with Glaze and decorate as below. Makes 5 to 5½ pounds fruitcake.

GLAZE

In small saucepan over low heat, melt ¼ cup *apple jelly;* brush over fruitcake. Decorate with flower designs made with *blanched whole almonds* for petals and *candied cherry* centers, pressing nuts and fruit firmly into glaze. Let glaze set before serving.

FABULOUS ENGLISH FRUITCAKE

3 cups all-purpose flour
½ teaspoon salt
1 teaspoon each ground cinnamon, nutmeg, allspice
1 tablespoon cocoa
16 ounces finely chopped
mixed candied fruits (3 cups)
1 15-ounce package golden raisins
1½ cups dark seedless raisins
2 cups dried currants
½ cup halved candied cherries
1½ cups butter or margarine
1½ cups packed dark brown sugar
2 tablespoons dark or light molasses
grated peel of 1 lemon and 1 orange
1½ cups blanched almonds, finely chopped
8 eggs
pale dry sherry or brandy
½ cup apricot preserves
Almond Paste (page 164)
Royal Icing (page 164)

One to 3 months before serving: Grease 9″ by 3″ springform pan. Pre-heat oven to 300° F. Into medium bowl, sift flour, salt, cinnamon, nutmeg, allspice and cocoa. In large bowl, mix candied fruits with next 4 ingredients.

In very large bowl, with electric mixer at medium speed, blend butter with sugar until light and fluffy. Add molasses, lemon and orange peels and almonds. Add 4 eggs, one at a time, beating well after each addition. Stir in ½ cup of the flour mixture. Add remaining 4 eggs, beating well after each. At low speed, beat in alternately, just until smooth, flour mixture and fruit mixture in thirds. When thoroughly blended, stir in ⅓ cup sherry. Turn into pan. With spoon, make hollow in center of batter so cake will rise evenly. Bake 3½ hours or until cake tester inserted in center comes out clean.

Cool cake in pan, on rack, for 2 hours. Remove cake from pan onto rack to cool completely. Wrap in foil and store at room temperature 1 week or longer. If desired, moisten with additional sherry.

Three days before serving: Melt apricot preserves; brush all over cake. Make Almond Paste. Divide almond paste in half. On waxed paper, lightly dusted with confectioners' sugar, roll one-half of paste to fit top of cake. If edges split, pinch together. With aid of waxed paper, flip almond paste onto top of cake; carefully remove paper. Gently press paste on cake.

Roll out other half of paste into two 14″ by 3″ strips. Wrap around cake. With fingers dipped in confectioners' sugar, press edges and seams together. Loosely wrap cake in foil; store at room temperature for one day before icing, to allow almond paste to dry.

Two days before serving: Make Royal Icing. Set cake on cake plate. Frost top with one-third of icing; smooth with wet spatula. Frost sides of cake with another third of icing; smooth. Let cake stand, uncovered, at room temperature for icing to dry, one day. Refrigerate rest of icing in tightly covered container overnight.

Day before serving: Remove icing from refrigerator to soften—do not uncover. Cut out 9-inch paper circle to fit top of cake. Fold in half 3 times to make 8 wedges. Place pattern on top of cake; secure at edges with 4 wooden picks. With straight pin, prick holes through pattern, into cake, to outline wedges. Remove wooden picks and pattern.

Use number 2 decorating tube in pastry bag. (If icing seems too firm, stir in a few drops of water before filling bag.) Outline each wedge with icing. Pipe a trellis in alternate wedges, making sure that the top lines cross the bottom lines at right angles; allow to dry.

Using small star or rosette tube, outline wedges and outer edge of top of cake with rosettes. Tint remaining icing green. With leaf tube, pipe row of leaves around underside of rosettes and around bottom edge of cake. With number 2 decorating tube, pipe red berry between each leaf. Allow cake to dry, uncovered, overnight. Makes 11 pounds fruit cake, enough for 40 servings. Use very sharp knife for easy slicing.

ALMOND PASTE*

Finely grind *four 4½-ounce cans blanched almonds.* Place in large bowl; set aside.

In double-boiler top, over hot, *not boiling,* water, beat *3 eggs* and *one 16-ounce package confectioners' sugar* until sugar is melted. Stir in *1 teaspoon almond extract* and *1 tablespoon lemon juice.* Remove from heat; pour over almonds; mix well. Sprinkle *confectioners' sugar* onto smooth surface; turn almond mixture onto it and knead until smooth, adding more confectioners' sugar if paste is too soft. Makes 2 pounds.

*Or use four 8-ounce cans almond paste.

ROYAL ICING

In large bowl, sift *2 pounds confectioners' sugar.* In another large bowl, combine *5 egg whites, 1 teaspoon lemon juice* and *5 or 6 drops glycerine* (from drug store) ; beat slightly. Add confectioners' sugar gradually, beating well with wooden spoon until icing is very white and forms stiff peaks, about 5 minutes. To keep icing from getting dry, cover bowl with damp cloth.

YELLOW LAYER CAKE

2½ cups cake flour, sifted before measuring
1½ cups granulated sugar
1 tablespoon double-acting baking powder
1 teaspoon salt
½ cup shortening
1 cup milk
1 teaspoon vanilla extract
2 eggs

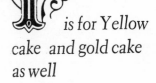

is for Yellow cake and gold cake as well

Early in day: Preheat oven to 375° F. Line two 8-inch layer-cake pans with waxed paper; grease paper.

Into large bowl, sift flour, sugar, baking powder and salt. With electric mixer at medium speed, beat in shortening, ⅔ cup of the milk and vanilla; beat 2 minutes, scraping bowl often. Add remaining ⅓ cup milk and the eggs; beat 2 minutes more. Divide batter evenly between the two pans. Bake 25 to 30 minutes or until done.

Cool layers in pans on racks 10 to 15 minutes. With spatula, loosen cake around edges; remove from pans; peel off waxed paper. Fill and frost with your favorite frosting. Makes 8 servings.

To vary: Bake in greased and floured 14″ by 10″ pan for ½ hour or until done. Cool, then sprinkle with *confectioners' sugar.* Serve, cut into diamonds.

MARBLE CAKE

2 17-ounce packages poundcake mix
⅓ cup cocoa
¼ teaspoon almond extract
confectioners' sugar

Day before: Grease and flour 10-inch bundt pan. Preheat oven and prepare cake mix as label directs. Into small bowl, pour 2 cups of the batter. In measuring cup, blend cocoa with ¼ cup cold water and almond extract; fold into the 2 cups of batter.

Into bundt pan, spoon 1 cup of the remaining batter; top with some of chocolate batter; repeat until both batters have been used up, ending with white batter. Bake 1 hour 15 minutes or until cake tester inserted in center comes out clean; cool in pan on rack 10 minutes; remove from pan; cool on rack. Wrap in foil. Store at room temperature.

To serve: Sprinkle top of cake with confectioners' sugar. Makes 12 servings.

WONDER GOLD CAKE

2¼ cups cake flour, sifted before measuring
2 teaspoons double-acting baking powder
¾ teaspoon salt
1 cup granulated sugar
½ teaspoon mace
½ cup shortening
5 egg yolks
1 teaspoon vanilla extract
or 2 teaspoons grated orange peel
¾ cup milk
confectioners' sugar

Early in day: Preheat oven to 350° F. Grease and line with waxed paper, bottom of 10" by 5" loaf pan.

Into large bowl, sift flour with baking powder, salt, sugar and mace. With electric mixer at low speed, beat in shortening, egg yolks, vanilla, and ½ cup of the milk until flour is dampened; beat 2 minutes at medium speed, scraping bowl and beaters as needed. Add remaining ¼ cup milk; beat 1 minute. Spoon into pan. Bake 1 hour or until cake tester inserted in center comes out clean. (Top of cake will crack.) Cool on rack for 10 minutes; remove from pan; peel off waxed paper; cool completely.

To serve: Sprinkle with confectioners' sugar. Makes 10 servings.

VENETIAN RUM CAKE
pictured between pages 144-145

1 18½-ounce package yellow-cake mix
1 14-ounce can sweetened condensed milk
1 tablespoon cornstarch
6 eggs, separated
vanilla extract
¼ cup rum
1 8-ounce jar mixed candied fruits
for cake, finely chopped
¾ cup finely chopped pecans
¾ cup granulated sugar

Day before serving: Preheat oven; prepare and bake cake mix as label directs in two 8-inch layer-cake pans; cool on racks.

Meanwhile, in double-boiler top, slowly stir condensed milk into the cornstarch. Add unbeaten egg yolks, stirring until smooth. (Cover egg whites and refrigerate.) Continuing to stir, slowly add 1⅓ cups hot water. Cook over boiling water, stirring constantly, until custard thickens, about 10 minutes. Remove from heat; stir in 1 teaspoon vanilla; pour into bowl; cover surface of custard with waxed paper; refrigerate.

With long sharp knife, split cooled layers in half, horizontally, making 4 layers in all. Sprinkle cut surface of each layer with 1 tablespoon of the rum.

Place one layer, cut side up, on heatproof platter. Spread with one third of the cold custard. Combine fruits and nuts; sprinkle one third of this mixture on top of custard. Repeat, using 2 more layers with remaining custard and fruit-nut mixture; top with fourth layer, cut side down; refrigerate.

About 3 hours before serving: Remove egg whites from refrigerator.

About 2 hours before serving: Preheat oven to 375° F. In large bowl, with electric mixer at high speed, beat egg whites until foamy; add 2 tablespoons of the sugar; beat at low speed 5 minutes, then at high speed 1 minute; repeat until all the sugar has been added. Stir in 1 teaspoon vanilla. Thickly swirl on top and sides of cake. Bake until meringue is golden, about 5 minutes. Cool, then refrigerate.

To serve: Dip long sharp knife into hot water, then cut cake into wedges. Makes 12 servings.

GERMAN GOLD-CAKE RING

3½ cups cake flour, sifted before measuring
1½ teaspoons double-acting baking powder
⅛ teaspoon salt
1 cup butter or margarine
2 cups granulated sugar
6 egg yolks
2 teaspoons vanilla extract
1 cup milk

Early in day: Preheat oven to 350° F. Sift together flour, baking powder, salt. Grease, then flour, 3-quart fluted ring mold.

In large bowl, with electric mixer at high speed, mix butter with sugar; gradually add egg yolks and vanilla, beating until very light and fluffy. At low speed, beat in alternately, until smooth, flour mixture in fourths, milk in thirds. Turn batter into ring mold. Bake 1 hour or until cake tester inserted in center comes out clean; cool in pan on rack 10 minutes; remove from pan; cool.

To serve: Serve sliced, as is. Or, if desired, fill center with scoops of ice cream; drizzle with caramel sauce. Makes 24 servings.

EASY PETITS FOURS
pictured between pages 144-145

1 18½-ounce package yellow-cake mix
¼ cup cocoa
¾ teaspoon baking soda
⅓ cup apricot preserves
⅓ cup raspberry jam
Chocolate Glaze (below)
Lemon Glaze (opposite)
candied cherries, citron, blanched slivered almonds,
flaked coconut, chocolate sprinkles
and semisweet-chocolate pieces for garnish
Coffee Frosting (opposite)
Almond Glaze (opposite)

Early in day: Grease and flour two 8-inch square pans. Preheat oven and prepare cake mix as label directs. Pour half of batter into one pan. To remaining batter, add cocoa mixed with soda and ¼ cup hot water; mix well. Pour into other pan. Bake and cool as label directs.

Split cakes in half horizontally; cut each cake into four 8″ by 4″ layers. Spread one yellow layer with apricot preserves, another with raspberry jam. Top with remaining yellow layers, cut side down. Frost top of apricot loaf with Chocolate Glaze, raspberry loaf with Lemon Glaze. With fork, mark lemon glaze as pictured; garnish with cherries and leaves of citron as pictured. Chill 1 hour or until glaze sets.

With knife, trim away any glaze that ran down sides of loaves. Brush long sides of apricot-filled loaf with apricot preserves; press almonds into preserves. Brush raspberry-filled loaf with raspberry jam; press coconut into jam. Refrigerate.

Spread two of the chocolate layers with Coffee Frosting; top with remaining chocolate layers, cut side down, making two loaves. Frost tops with Almond Glaze; chill 1 hour or until frosting is set.

With knife, trim away any glaze that ran down sides of loaves. Spread long sides with remaining Coffee Frosting. Place chocolate sprinkles on waxed paper. Press frosted sides of loaves into sprinkles to coat evenly. Arrange semisweet-chocolate on top as pictured. Chill.

To serve: Cut loaves into 1-inch slices. Makes 16 servings.

CHOCOLATE GLAZE

In bowl, beat *½ cup plus 2 tablespoons sifted confectioners' sugar, 1½ teaspoons chocolate-flavored quick-milk mix, ¾ teaspoon orange juice and 2 teaspoons hot water* until smooth and spreadable.

LEMON GLAZE

In bowl, beat ¾ *cup sifted confectioners' sugar* with ¾ *teaspoon lemon juice* and 2½ *teaspoons hot water* until smooth and spreadable.

COFFEE FROSTING

In bowl, beat *1 cup butter or margarine*, softened, until light and fluffy. Gradually beat in *1 cup sifted confectioners' sugar*. Dissolve *1 tablespoon instant coffee* in *1 tablespoon hot water*; beat into frosting.

ALMOND GLAZE

In bowl, stir *1½ cups sifted confectioners' sugar* with *2 drops almond extract* and *about 2 tablespoons hot water* until spreadable.

TWIN PETITS FOURS
pictured between pages 144-145

1 18½-ounce package yellow-cake mix
1½ cups butter or margarine
1 1-pound package confectioners' sugar, sifted
2 teaspoons grated orange peel
2 teaspoons orange juice
1 8-ounce can mandarin-orange sections, drained
¼ cup chopped blanched almonds
2 teaspoons instant coffee
walnut halves

Early in day: Preheat oven; prepare and bake cake mix as label directs in greased and floured 9-inch square pan. Cool as directed. Split cake in half horizontally, then cut into four 9″ by 4½″ layers.

In large mixing bowl, with electric mixer at medium speed, cream butter until light and fluffy; gradually beat in 3 cups of sugar until well blended. Divide this butter cream in half. To one half, add ¼ cup sugar, orange peel and juice; mix well. Spread one layer with one-third of this orange butter cream; top with another layer, cut side down. Frost top and long sides with remaining orange butter cream; with fork, mark top as pictured and garnish with orange sections. Press almonds into frosting on sides of loaf; refrigerate.

Dissolve coffee in 1 tablespoon hot water; add to remaining half of butter cream with ⅓ cup sugar; mix well. Spread another layer with one-third of this mixture; top with remaining layer, cut side down. Frost top and long sides with remaining coffee mixture. Arrange 9 walnuts down center of loaf; place more on sides. Refrigerate.

To serve: Cut cakes into 1-inch slices. Makes 18 servings.

GEORGE WASHINGTON'S CAKE

1½ cups cake flour, sifted before measuring
2 teaspoons double-acting baking powder
¼ teaspoon salt
¾ cup granulated sugar
⅓ cup butter or margarine, softened
1 teaspoon vanilla extract
2 eggs
½ cup milk
1 10-ounce jar red-raspberry preserves
confectioners' sugar

is for Zabaglione, fitting end to a meal

Early in day: Grease two 8-inch layer-cake pans. Preheat oven to 375° F.
Sift flour with baking powder and salt. In bowl, with electric mixer at medium speed, cream sugar, butter and vanilla; beat in eggs. At low speed, alternately beat in milk and flour mixture. Pour into pans; bake 25 minutes or until cake tester inserted in center comes out clean. Cool on rack; remove from pans; cool completely. Spread preserves between layers. Dust top with confectioners' sugar. Makes 12 servings.

ZABAGLIONE

3 egg yolks, slightly beaten
¾ cup granulated sugar
2 teaspoons grated lemon peel
5 teaspoons lemon juice
½ cup sherry or Marsala wine

Just before serving: In double-boiler top, combine all ingredients. Cook over boiling water, beating constantly with rotary beater, until as thick and fluffy as whipped cream. Remove from water at once. Serve hot in sherbet, parfait or champagne glasses. Makes 4 servings.

FRUITED: Serve hot, over dishes of *strawberries, raspberries, peach slices,* drained *canned fruit cocktail, sliced oranges, sliced pineapple* or *banana chunks.* Makes 6 servings.

PÊCHES SULTANES: About 1 hour before serving, cook as above, but use *2 egg yolks, 3 tablespoons sugar* and *2½ tablespoons Chablis;* omit lemon peel and juice. Add *1 teaspoon Cointreau* if desired. When thick and fluffy, set top in ice water; beat until cool. Serve over *peach slices.* Makes 2 servings.

INDEX